SAVING THE WORLD...
ONE IDEA AT A TIME!

HOWTOONS [RE]IGNITION

HOWTOONS created by *Dr. Saul Griffith, Nick Dragotta, & Joost Bonsen.*

- Writer: **Fred Van Lente**
- Artist: **Tom Fowler**
- Colors: **Jordie Bellaire**
- Letters: **Rus Wooton**
- Project Design: **Ingrid Dragotta**
- Coordinated by: HOWTOONS

PLEASE NOTE: THE AUTHORS & PUBLISHER RECOMMEND ADULT SUPERVISION ON ALL PROJECTS!

!

The authors and publisher of HOWTOONS have made every reasonable effort to ensure projects and activities contained in this book are safe when conducted as instructed, but assume no responsibility for any injuries suffered or damages or losses incurred as a result of following the instructions contained in this book.

HOWTOONS [RE]IGNITION, VOL. 1. First printing. March 2015. **Published by Image Comics, Inc.** Office of publication: 2001 Center Street, Sixth Floor, Berkeley, CA 94704. Originally published in single magazine form as Howtoons [Re]Ignition #1-5, by Image Comics. Printed in the USA. For information regarding the CPSIA on this printed material call: 203-595-3636 and provide reference #RICH–605761. For international rights, contact: foreignlicensing@imagecomics.com. ISBN: 978-1-63215-056-1

1

PROLOGUE:
[PRE]IGNITION

WHERE?
92,960,000 MILES AWAY.*

WHEN?
EIGHT MINUTES AGO!

WHAT?!?!

* OR 149,600,000 KILOMETERS.

Energy, THAT'S WHAT -- THE ABILITY OF A SYSTEM TO DO WORK!
"WORK" IN THIS INSTANCE IS EXERTING FORCE ON ANOTHER SYSTEM FROM A DISTANCE --
-- EVEN A HUGE DISTANCE LIKE THAT BETWEEN EARTH AND OUR SUN!
THAT FORCE TRANSFERS ENERGY FROM ONE SYSTEM TO ANOTHER -- LIKE LIGHT FROM A SUN TO A PLANET!
THAT LIGHT TAKES EIGHT MINUTES AT THE SPEED OF, UH, Y'KNOW, LIGHT, TO REACH EARTH ... BUT NOT ALL OF IT MAKES IT TO THE PLANET'S SURFACE.
A LOT OF IT BOUNCES OFF THE UPPER PART OF THE ATMOSPHERE--
-- AND MORE GETS ABSORBED ON THE WAY DOWN BY A MOTLEY CREW OF WATER VAPOR, CARBON DIOXIDE, METHANE, NITROUS OXIDE, AND OZONE -- WHAT WE LIKE TO CALL "THE GREENHOUSE GANG!"
LIGHT ABSORBED BY GREENHOUSE GASES WARMS THE EARTH -- AND THIS, AMONG MANY OTHER FACTORS, IS WHAT MAKES OUR PLANET IDEAL FOR SUPPORTING LIFE!

PLANTS EVOLVED TO TRANSFORM SOME OF THE LIGHT THAT ESCAPES THE GREENHOUSE LAYER INTO SUGARS AND CARBOHYDRATES VIA PHOTOSYNTHESIS!
(THAT'S -- YES -- ANOTHER TRANSFER OF ENERGY BETWEEN SYSTEMS!)
ANIMALS EVOLVED TO CAPTURE THOSE STORED NUTRIENTS FOR THEMSELVES BY EATING SAID PLANTS!
(...AND ANOTHER TRANSFER...)
OTHER ANIMALS EVOLVED TO SNAG THOSE NUTRIENTS FOR THEMSELVES BY EATING THOSE ANIMALS!
ALL THIS ENERGY -- FROM THAT SINGLE BEAM OF SUNLIGHT!

BUT IT DOESN'T END THERE!
THAT ENERGY INSIDE PLANTS AND ANIMALS DOESN'T JUST VANISH WHEN THEY DIE.
TRAPPED MILLIONS OF YEARS IN THE GROUND, THOSE BIOLOGICAL MATERIALS TRANSFORM INTO A RICH VARIETY OF HYDROCARBONS.
HUMANS LEARNED HOW TO HARNESS THESE "FOSSIL FUELS" IN THE 19TH AND 20TH CENTURIES...
DINOSAUR
ENERGY

...AND IGNITED THE FIRE OF TECHNOLOGICAL ADVANCEMENT THAT BUILT THE MODERN WORLD AS WE KNOW IT TODAY!
DINOSAUR ENERGY
YOON
Vote Now!
BUT NO FORM OF ENERGY EVER DISAPPEARS ENTIRELY.
THE INEFFICIENT BURNING OF THOSE FUELS RELEASES GREENHOUSE GASES (OR CHEMICALS) INTO THE ATMOSPHERE -- BULKING UP THE GREENHOUSE LAYER --
-- WITH CONSEQUENCES UNIMAGINABLE TO THOSE WHO FIRST PULLED OIL, COAL AND NATURAL GAS FROM THE EARTH!

KRAKKATHOOOOM

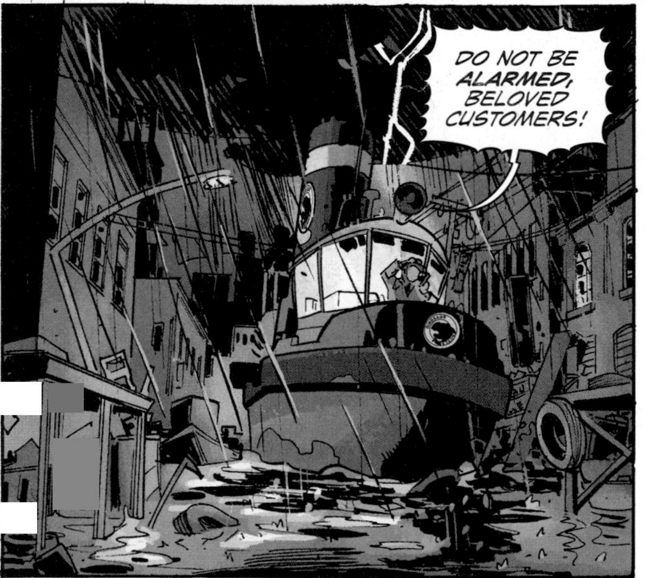
DO NOT BE ALARMED, BELOVED CUSTOMERS!

YOU ARE ABOUT TO HEAR AN EXTREMELY LARGE EXPLOSION!
THAT'S JUST YOUR FRIENDS AT DINOSAUR ENERGY ATTEMPTING TO GEO-ENGINEER THE EARTH'S CLIMATE!

WE MUST PROTECT OUR PLANET FROM THAT TRAITOR, THE SUN!

AND WE SHALL DO SO BY ENLISTING THE AID OF MANKIND'S BEST FRIEND -- OUR MIGHTY VOLCANOES!

AWRIGHT -- LET THEM NUKES DROP!

WE SHALL PURPOSEFULLY BLOW THEM UP SO THEY MAY COVER THE GLOBE IN A PROTECTIVE LAYER OF ASH AND DEFLECT EVEN MORE LIGHT FROM THE ATMOSPHERE!

IT'S LIKE THE EARTH IS GIVING HERSELF A HUG! AWWWW!
AND IT'S THE ONLY WAY (WE CAN THINK OF) TO SLOW DOWN GLOBAL WARMING, WITH ITS FREAKY WEATHER AND RISING SEA LEVELS --

-- WHICH OUR LAWYERS TELL US WE HUMANS HAD NOTHING TO DO WITH WHATSOEVER!
NOPE! UH-UH! WASN'T US! IT WAS LIKE THIS WHEN WE GOT HERE!

BUT, UH... YOU'RE PROBABLY GONNA WANNA COVER YOUR EARS!
IN, LIKE... T-MINUS 3 MINUTES!

HEY!
AWWW YEAH! ANOTHER CORPSE-MUNCHER BITES THE GRAVEDUST!
POK

TUCK?! WHAT'S THE BIG IDEA?
DIDN'T YOU HEAR THE MAN WITH THE BIG VOICE, CELINE? THE ZOMBIE APOCALYPSE IS COMING--
--AND I'VE GOT TO PRACTICE MY AIM!

NOT THAT, BRAIN-ROT!

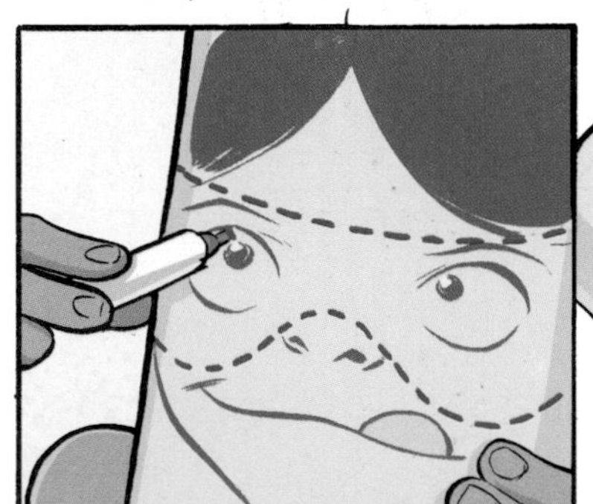

TRACE THE OUTLINE FOR THE MASK ON YOUR FACE!

CUT AGAIN! **CAREFULLY** MAKE TWO SLITS IN EACH CORNER WITH A HOBBY KNIFE!

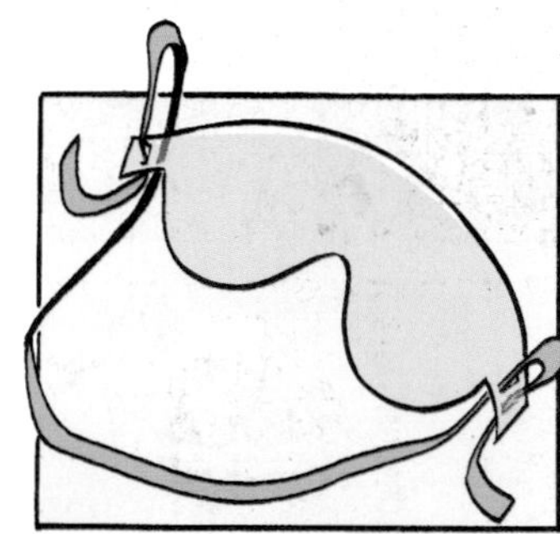

THREAD THE **STRAP** (USE PART OF A BIKE INNER TUBE; OR TIE RUBBER BANDS TOGETHER) THROUGH THE FOUR SLITS!

WARNING: THESE GOGGLES ARE TOYS AND WILL PROTECT YOUR EYES ONLY AGAINST MARSHMALLOWS. NEVER SUBSTITUTE THEM FOR CERTIFIED SAFETY GLASSES WHEN RECOMMENDED.

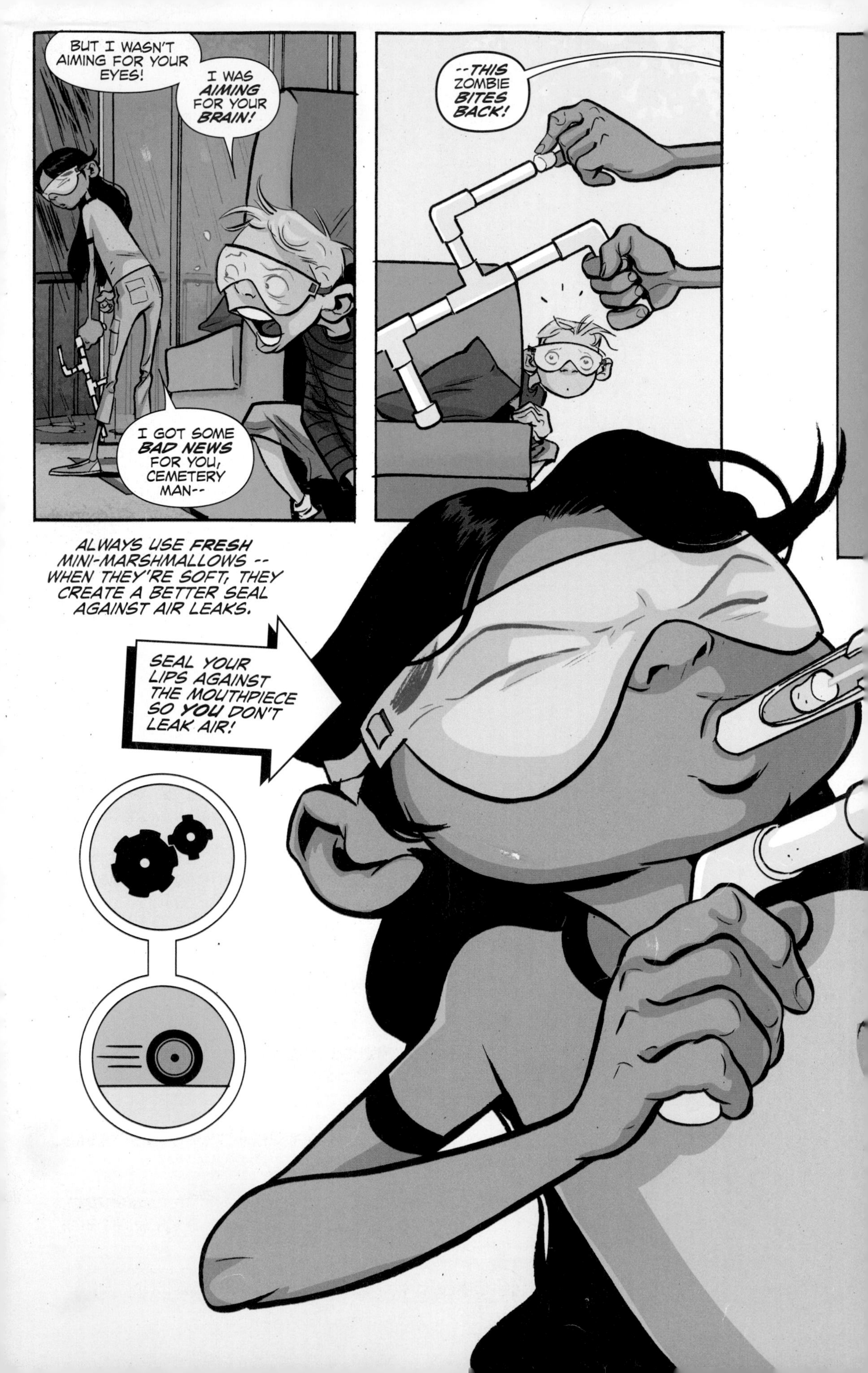
BUT I WASN'T AIMING FOR YOUR EYES!
I WAS AIMING FOR YOUR BRAIN!
I GOT SOME BAD NEWS FOR YOU, CEMETERY MAN--
--THIS ZOMBIE BITES BACK!
ALWAYS USE FRESH MINI-MARSHMALLOWS -- WHEN THEY'RE SOFT, THEY CREATE A BETTER SEAL AGAINST AIR LEAKS.
SEAL YOUR LIPS AGAINST THE MOUTHPIECE SO YOU DON'T LEAK AIR!

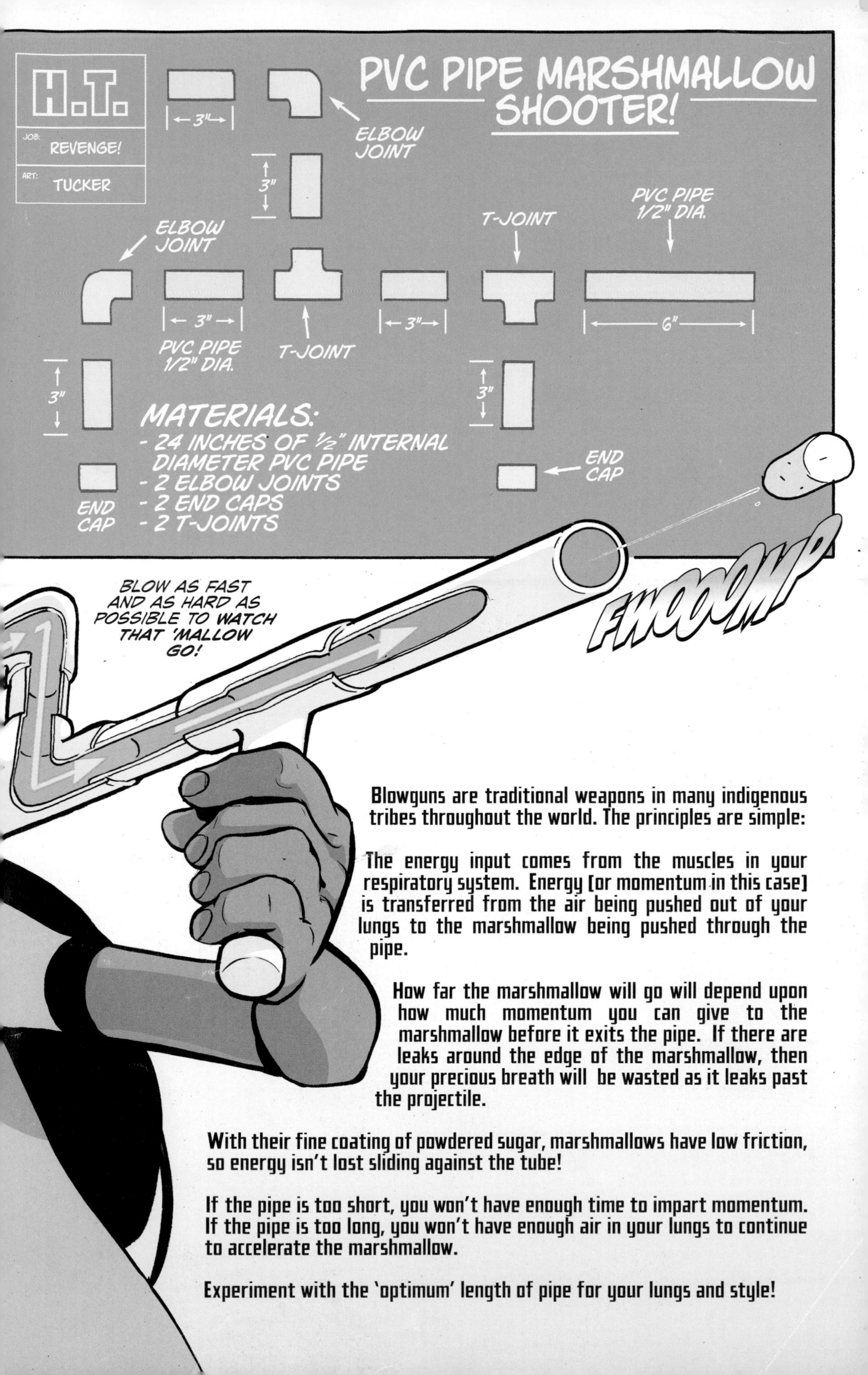

Blowguns are traditional weapons in many indigenous tribes throughout the world. The principles are simple:

The energy input comes from the muscles in your respiratory system. Energy [or momentum in this case] is transferred from the air being pushed out of your lungs to the marshmallow being pushed through the pipe.

How far the marshmallow will go will depend upon how much momentum you can give to the marshmallow before it exits the pipe. If there are leaks around the edge of the marshmallow, then your precious breath will be wasted as it leaks past the projectile.

With their fine coating of powdered sugar, marshmallows have low friction, so energy isn't lost sliding against the tube!

If the pipe is too short, you won't have enough time to impart momentum. If the pipe is too long, you won't have enough air in your lungs to continue to accelerate the marshmallow.

Experiment with the 'optimum' length of pipe for your lungs and style!

MOAH WIKE DIII OMBUH HUULL OHH HOOB AIIHHH
WHAT?!
FWOOOOMP

"MORE LIKE THIS ZOMBIE IS FULL OF HOT AIR!" HAH!
POINK
POINK

OKAY, TUCK, CELINE -- PLAYTIME'S OVER ... MAYBE FOREVER.
LET'S GO, WE'RE OUT OF TIME --
AW, C'MON, MA -- THIS IS IMPORTANT "DOOMSDAY TRAINING!"

ONLY IF POST-APOCALYPTIC WARFARE WILL BE WAGED WITH A DESSERT TREAT.
OH, LIKE YOU KNOW IT WON'T!
NO MORE EXCUSES -- SUIT UP!

MOM, DAD -- ARE YOU SURE WE HAVE TO DO THIS? WHAT ABOUT MY FRIENDS -- MY SCHOOL?
WE HAVE FRIENDS TOO, HONEY -- AND WORK WE'RE LEAVING BEHIND!
YOUR FATHER AND I TOLD DINOSAUR ENERGY THIS WAS A STUPID PLAN -- BUT IF THEY WON'T LISTEN TO THEIR TOP SCIENTISTS, WHAT ELSE CAN WE DO?
GEE, I DON'T KNOW ... LIKE, CONVINCE PEOPLE THERE'S A BETTER WAY?

MAYBE YOU'RE RIGHT. ACTUALLY, I'M SURE YOU'RE RIGHT.
BUT YOU'LL LEARN, CELINE. BEING RIGHT DOESN'T MATTER WHEN YOU'RE OUT OF TIME.
JUST -- PROMISE ME SOMETHING, CELINE.

YOU'RE SMART -- MAYBE TOO SMART FOR YOUR OWN GOOD, SOMETIMES.
JUST -- IF ANYTHING HAPPENS -- TO YOUR FATHER OR ME, IN THE MIDDLE OF THIS CRAZINESS--

WHAT ... WHAT'S GOING TO HAPPEN TO YOU?
NOTHING. I HOPE.
BUT -- WATCH AFTER YOUR BROTHER. HE DOESN'T HAVE THE SELF-CONTROL YOU DO.
BUT MOOOOOM -- HE'S NOT MY REAL --

PROMISE.
OKAY, OKAY. GEEZ. I PROMISE.

YOU'RE -- SCARING ME...
I'M SORRY, HONEY...
...MAYBE I SHOULD HAVE SCARED YOU MORE, SOONER...

T-MINUS 30 SECONDS ... GET YOUR CELL PHONES AND CAMERAS READY! YOU'RE NOT GONNA WANNA MISS THIS!
OKAY, N.A.N.N.I....
TEN SECONDS BEFORE THE BIG SHOW!
ALL PAID FOR BY A MINOR SURCHARGE ON YOUR ENERGY BILL, ALL THANKS TO YOUR GOOD BUDDIES AT DINO-E!

...TAKE US DOWN.

THREE,
TWO,
ONE!
SHOWTI-

ROKAKRKOKAWHOOOOOOOOM

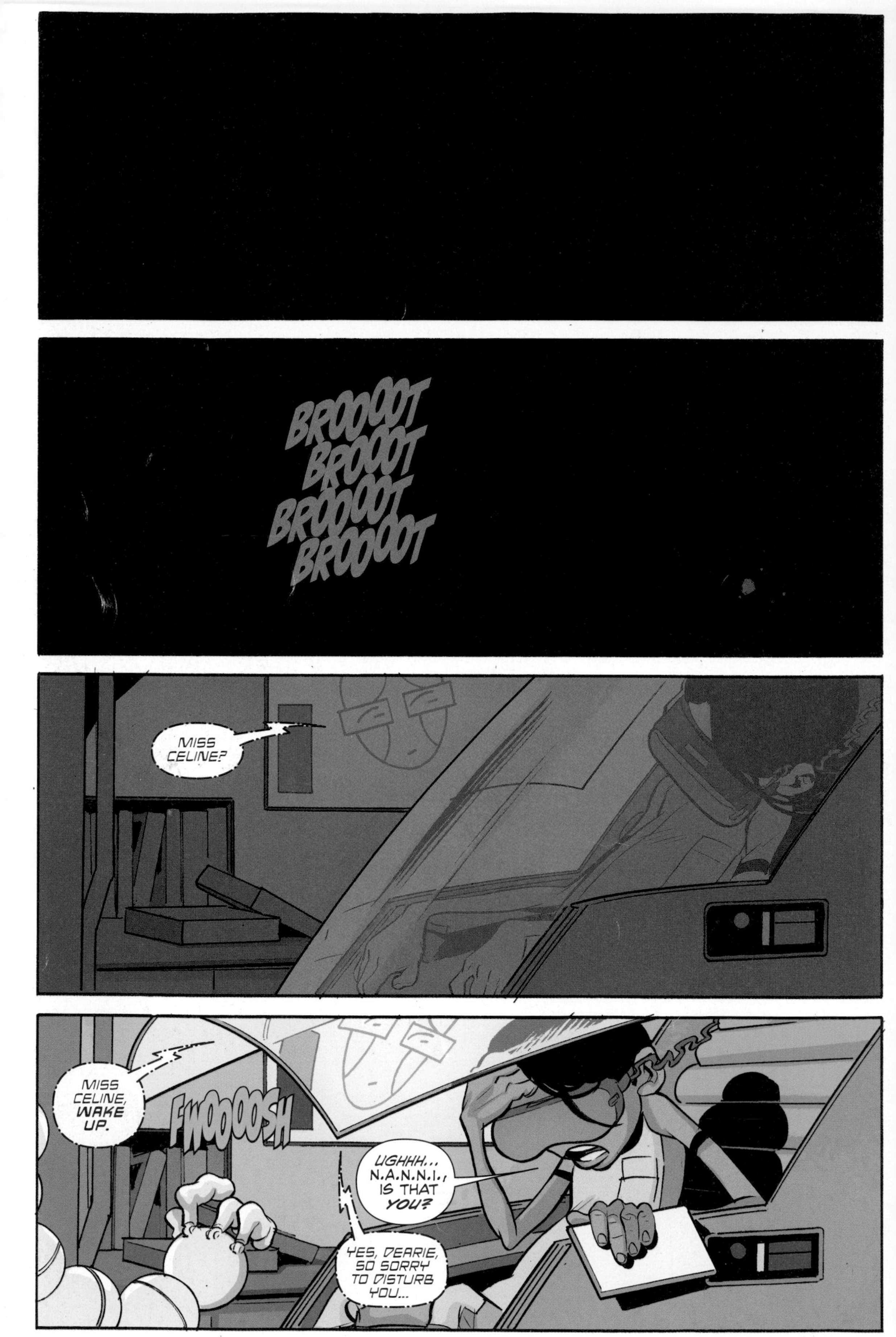
BROOOOT
BROOOT
BROOOOT
BROOOOT
MISS CELINE?
MISS CELINE, WAKE UP.
FWOOOOSH
UGHHH... N.A.N.N.I., IS THAT YOU?
YES, DEARIE, SO SORRY TO DISTURB YOU...

...AND INTERRUPT YOUR LESSONS...
DREAMSCHOOL®
ENERGY MODULE

...BUT WE'RE IN SOMETHING OF A STICKY WICKET...
WHAT IS IT? WHAT'S HAPPENING? DO MOM AND DAD KNOW?

ONLY... FRAG... TWO HUNDRED AND TWELVE MORE ZOMBIES... SNORK... GET THE HUMONGOUS BOOMSTICK®™...
BLEEP BOOP BANG

TUCK!!
AAAHHH! WHAT IS IT? WHAT'S THE PROBLEM?

NOW THAT YOU'RE FINALLY AWAKE WE CAN FIND OUT!

OUR EMERGENCY RESERVE POWER IS DOWN TO TWENTY-FIVE PERCENT! IT WILL NOT BE LONG BEFORE BUNKER SYSTEMS ARE RENDERED NON-OPERATIONAL.
YOUR PARENTS MADE THEIR CALCULATIONS AS BEST THEY COULD, BUT THERE WAS AN UNANTICIPATED DRAIN ON OUR RESOURCES.
WHAT? WE'RE OUT OF FUEL? HOW IS THAT POSSIBLE?
WELL -- OKAY. OKAY...
WHAT DO MOM AND DAD THINK WE SHOULD DO?
SCRATCH SCRATCH

THAT'S ... THAT'S JUST IT.
I AWOKE YOUR PARENTS AND INFORMED THEM OF OUR SITUATION A WEEK AGO.
THEY TOOK THE BUNKER'S ROVER AND VENTURED OUT IN SEARCH OF MORE FUEL...
...AND NEVER RETURNED.
MOM
DAD
THEY'RE ... THEY'RE GONE? HOW MUCH LONGER CAN WE STAY DOWN HERE?!

IF I DIVERTED ALL THE POWER TO THE LIFE SUPPORT SYSTEMS. WE SHOULD HAVE ENOUGH TO KEEP YOU IN CLEAN AIR FOR FIVE DAYS...
THREE DAYS...

TWELVE HOURS...

SIX HOURS...
WAIT! STOP! WHAT'S DRAINING ALL OUR POWER?!

HEY, CELINE, THIS PLACE IS GREAT! HOW LONG DO WE GET TO STAY HERE?
DAAAAAGGHHHH!
WAAAAAAAAAA
WHRRRRRR
BRUSH BRUSH BRUSH
BEEP BOOP
BANG BANG BANG BANG
UNPLUG ALL THAT STUFF! TURN IT ALL OFF! WE GOTTA CONSERVE OUR POWER!

WHY? HOW MUCH DO WE HAVE LEFT?
NOT ENOUGH.

OOOOOH BOY.

KLONK
REND
SQUEEE
RENCH RENCH
HUBBA HUBBA
TUCK, WHAT ARE YOU DOING?
RENCH RENCH
SQUEEEKLONK
REND
KLONK
BREAKING DOWN THESE GADGETS INTO PIECES-PARTS, SIS...
REND REND HUBBA
RENCH RENCH

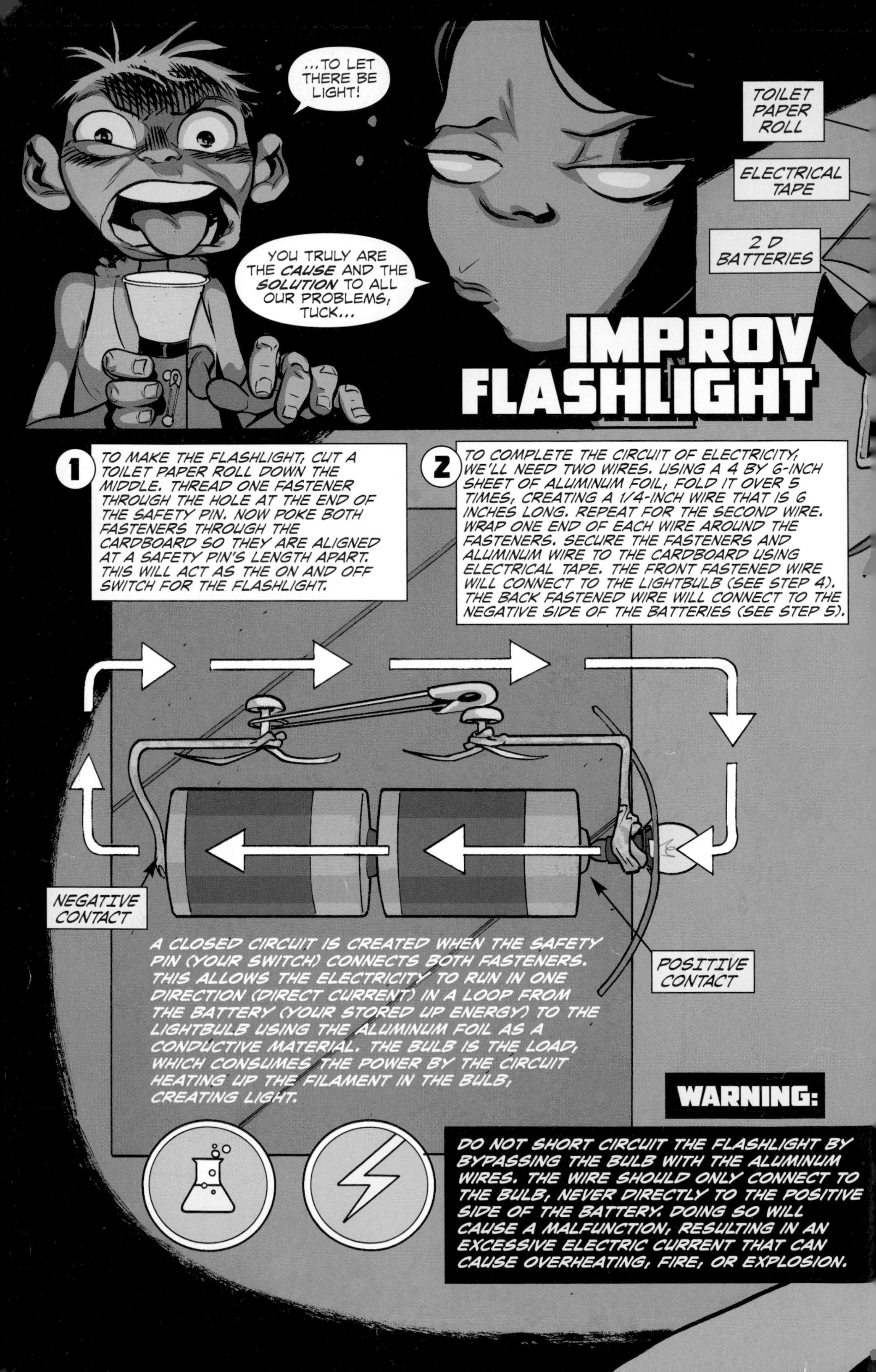
...TO LET THERE BE LIGHT!
YOU TRULY ARE THE CAUSE AND THE SOLUTION TO ALL OUR PROBLEMS, TUCK...
TOILET PAPER ROLL
ELECTRICAL TAPE
2 D BATTERIES
IMPROV FLASHLIGHT
1 TO MAKE THE FLASHLIGHT, CUT A TOILET PAPER ROLL DOWN THE MIDDLE. THREAD ONE FASTENER THROUGH THE HOLE AT THE END OF THE SAFETY PIN. NOW POKE BOTH FASTENERS THROUGH THE CARDBOARD SO THEY ARE ALIGNED AT A SAFETY PIN'S LENGTH APART. THIS WILL ACT AS THE ON AND OFF SWITCH FOR THE FLASHLIGHT.
2 TO COMPLETE THE CIRCUIT OF ELECTRICITY, WE'LL NEED TWO WIRES. USING A 4 BY 6-INCH SHEET OF ALUMINUM FOIL, FOLD IT OVER 5 TIMES, CREATING A 1/4-INCH WIRE THAT IS 6 INCHES LONG. REPEAT FOR THE SECOND WIRE. WRAP ONE END OF EACH WIRE AROUND THE FASTENERS. SECURE THE FASTENERS AND ALUMINUM WIRE TO THE CARDBOARD USING ELECTRICAL TAPE. THE FRONT FASTENED WIRE WILL CONNECT TO THE LIGHTBULB (SEE STEP 4). THE BACK FASTENED WIRE WILL CONNECT TO THE NEGATIVE SIDE OF THE BATTERIES (SEE STEP 5).
NEGATIVE CONTACT
POSITIVE CONTACT
A CLOSED CIRCUIT IS CREATED WHEN THE SAFETY PIN (YOUR SWITCH) CONNECTS BOTH FASTENERS. THIS ALLOWS THE ELECTRICITY TO RUN IN ONE DIRECTION (DIRECT CURRENT) IN A LOOP FROM THE BATTERY (YOUR STORED UP ENERGY) TO THE LIGHTBULB USING THE ALUMINUM FOIL AS A CONDUCTIVE MATERIAL. THE BULB IS THE LOAD, WHICH CONSUMES THE POWER BY THE CIRCUIT HEATING UP THE FILAMENT IN THE BULB, CREATING LIGHT.
WARNING:
DO NOT SHORT CIRCUIT THE FLASHLIGHT BY BYPASSING THE BULB WITH THE ALUMINUM WIRES. THE WIRE SHOULD ONLY CONNECT TO THE BULB, NEVER DIRECTLY TO THE POSITIVE SIDE OF THE BATTERY. DOING SO WILL CAUSE A MALFUNCTION, RESULTING IN AN EXCESSIVE ELECTRIC CURRENT THAT CAN CAUSE OVERHEATING, FIRE, OR EXPLOSION.

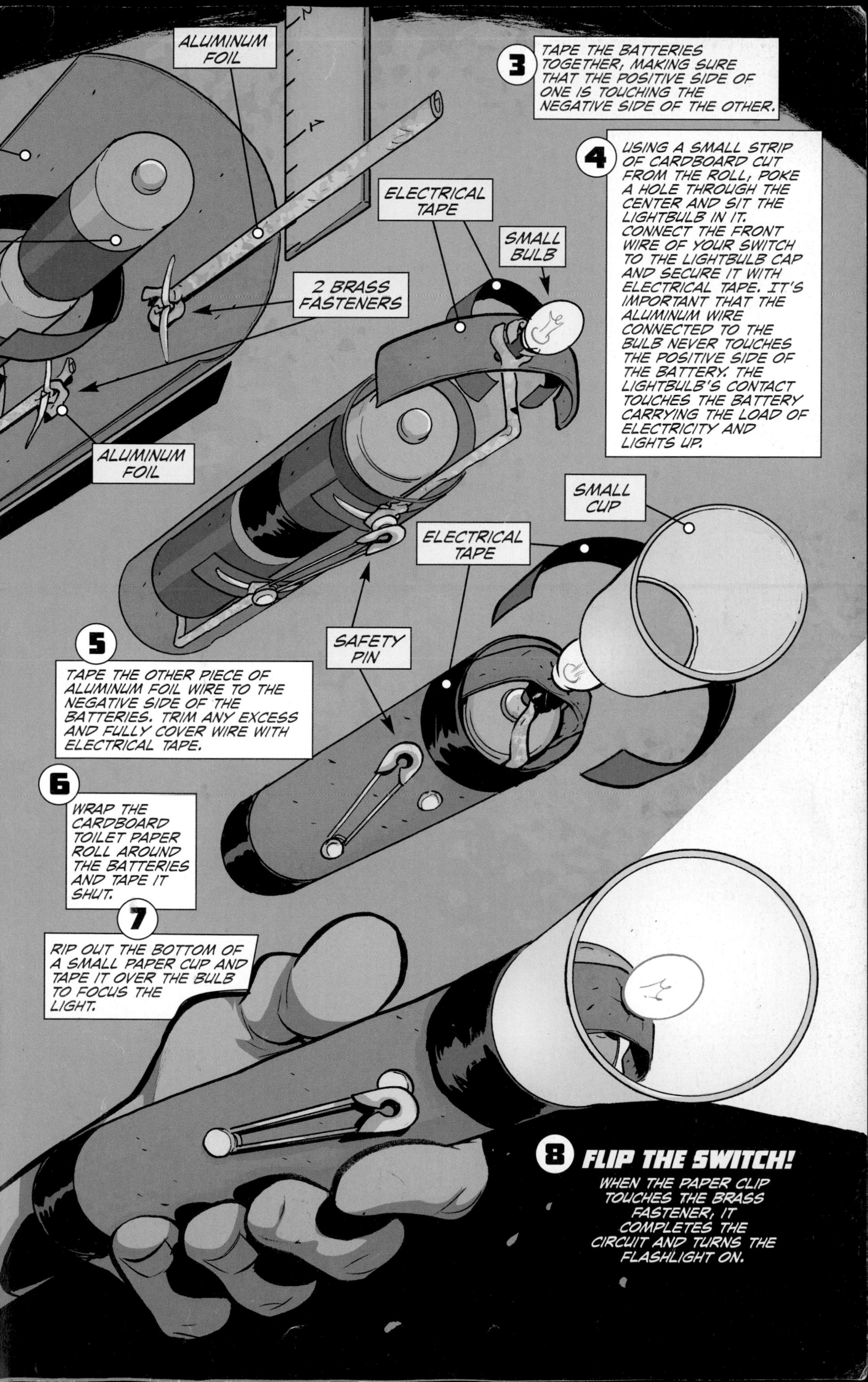
ALUMINUM FOIL
3 TAPE THE BATTERIES TOGETHER, MAKING SURE THAT THE POSITIVE SIDE OF ONE IS TOUCHING THE NEGATIVE SIDE OF THE OTHER.
4 USING A SMALL STRIP OF CARDBOARD CUT FROM THE ROLL, POKE A HOLE THROUGH THE CENTER AND SIT THE LIGHTBULB IN IT. CONNECT THE FRONT WIRE OF YOUR SWITCH TO THE LIGHTBULB CAP AND SECURE IT WITH ELECTRICAL TAPE. IT'S IMPORTANT THAT THE ALUMINUM WIRE CONNECTED TO THE BULB NEVER TOUCHES THE POSITIVE SIDE OF THE BATTERY. THE LIGHTBULB'S CONTACT TOUCHES THE BATTERY CARRYING THE LOAD OF ELECTRICITY AND LIGHTS UP.
ELECTRICAL TAPE
SMALL BULB
2 BRASS FASTENERS
ALUMINUM FOIL
SMALL CUP
ELECTRICAL TAPE
SAFETY PIN
5 TAPE THE OTHER PIECE OF ALUMINUM FOIL WIRE TO THE NEGATIVE SIDE OF THE BATTERIES. TRIM ANY EXCESS AND FULLY COVER WIRE WITH ELECTRICAL TAPE.
6 WRAP THE CARDBOARD TOILET PAPER ROLL AROUND THE BATTERIES AND TAPE IT SHUT.
7 RIP OUT THE BOTTOM OF A SMALL PAPER CUP AND TAPE IT OVER THE BULB TO FOCUS THE LIGHT.
8 FLIP THE SWITCH!
WHEN THE PAPER CLIP TOUCHES THE BRASS FASTENER, IT COMPLETES THE CIRCUIT AND TURNS THE FLASHLIGHT ON.

C'MON =GASP= WITHOUT POWER, THE PUMPS WON'T BE ABLE TO GET US =WHEEZE= AIR TO BREATHE FROM OUTSIDE!
BUT =KOFF= WHAT ABOUT MOM AND DAD? WE JUST CAN'T =GAK= LEAVE THEM BEHIND!

THAT'S JUST IT! THEY'VE ALREADY =KOFF= GONE!
WHADAYOU MEAN =CHOKE= GONE?

I'LL EXPLAIN =HUFF= WHEN WE'RE OUTSIDE!

WAIT, MOM AND DAD SAID...
...NEVER TO DO THAT...

YEAH, I KNOW. BUT THEY'RE NOT HERE ANYMORE.
WE'RE GONNA FIND THEM -- BUT WE GOTTA STICK TOGETHER TO DO IT. OKAY, TUCK?
WHO KNOWS HOW LONG WE'VE BEEN ASLEEP -- WHO KNOWS WHAT WE'RE GONNA FIND OUT THERE.

ONLY THING WE CAN COUNT ON IS EACH OTHER.
YOU WITH ME, TUCKER?
YEAH -- YEAH. OKAY, SIS. YOU CAN COUNT ON ME.
LET'S DO THIS.

KREEK--RRRRRRREEEEEEEEEE

WHOA...

...IT'S BEAUTIFUL...

3/13

Z

THERE'RE THE ROVER TRACKS -- HEADING TOWARD THE CITY IN THE DISTANCE... LET'S GO!

CELINE...
WHAT?
ARE YOU SURE WE'LL FIND MOM AND DAD THERE?

BRIGHT DAYS AH
I DON'T KNOW, TUCK. I'M NOT SURE OF ANYTHING.
OKAY...
WE HAVE TO START LOOKING SOMEWHERE.

WERE YOU ABLE TO GRAB ANYTHING FROM THE BUNKER BEFORE WE LEFT?
THE ONLY THING IN MY POCKET IS A STUPID PACKET OF PEANUTS.

PEANUTS AREN'T STUPID! THEY'RE ENERGY.
I THOUGHT THEY WERE FOOD.
SAME DIFFERENCE!

IN A WAY, IT EMBODIES EVERY DIFFERENT KIND OF ENERGY!

POTENTIAL (or "STORED") ENERGY

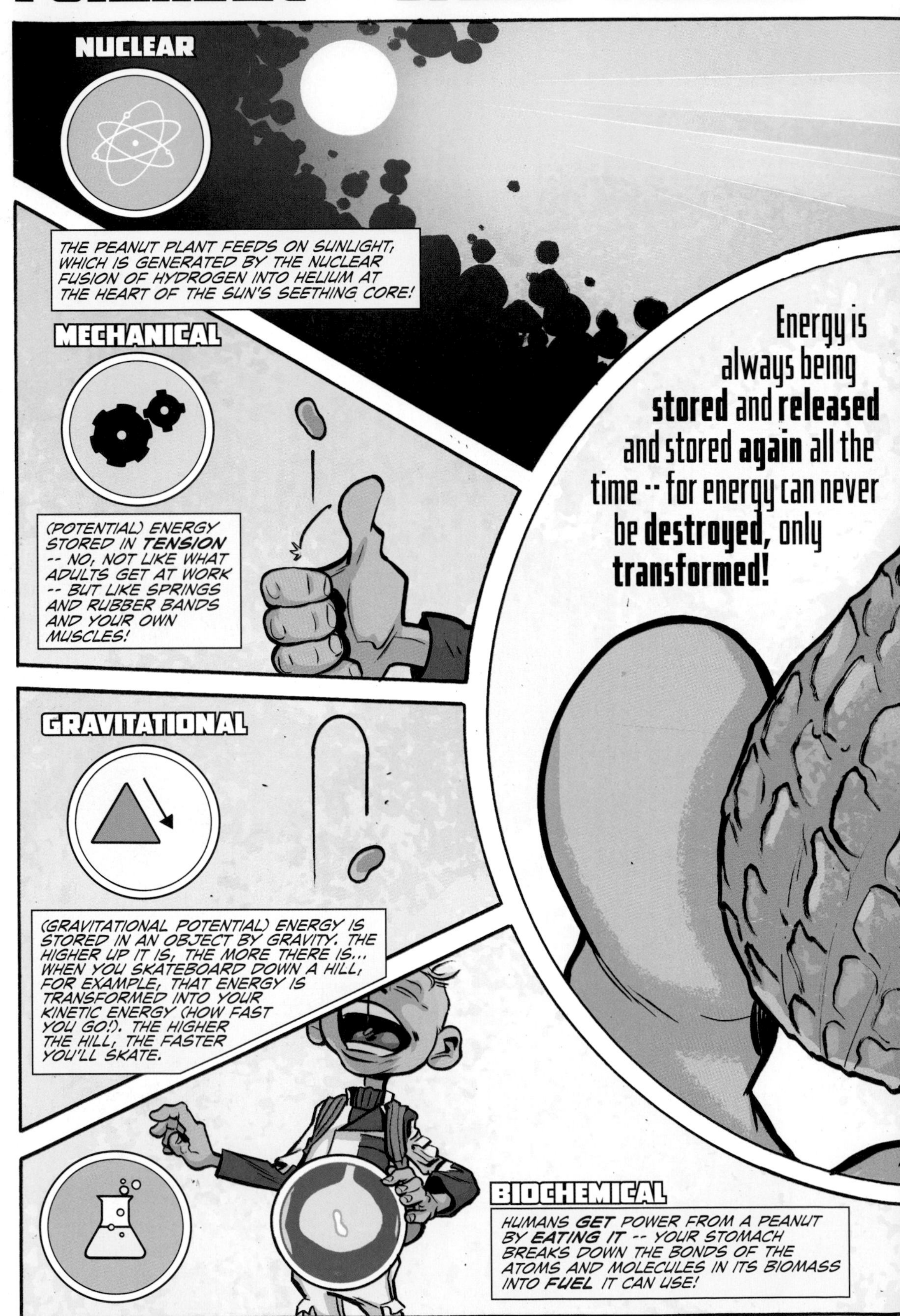

NUCLEAR
THE PEANUT PLANT FEEDS ON SUNLIGHT, WHICH IS GENERATED BY THE NUCLEAR FUSION OF HYDROGEN INTO HELIUM AT THE HEART OF THE SUN'S SEETHING CORE!
MECHANICAL
(POTENTIAL) ENERGY STORED IN TENSION -- NO, NOT LIKE WHAT ADULTS GET AT WORK -- BUT LIKE SPRINGS AND RUBBER BANDS AND YOUR OWN MUSCLES!
Energy is always being stored and released and stored again all the time -- for energy can never be destroyed, only transformed!
GRAVITATIONAL
(GRAVITATIONAL POTENTIAL) ENERGY IS STORED IN AN OBJECT BY GRAVITY. THE HIGHER UP IT IS, THE MORE THERE IS... WHEN YOU SKATEBOARD DOWN A HILL, FOR EXAMPLE, THAT ENERGY IS TRANSFORMED INTO YOUR KINETIC ENERGY (HOW FAST YOU GO!). THE HIGHER THE HILL, THE FASTER YOU'LL SKATE.
BIOCHEMICAL
HUMANS GET POWER FROM A PEANUT BY EATING IT -- YOUR STOMACH BREAKS DOWN THE BONDS OF THE ATOMS AND MOLECULES IN ITS BIOMASS INTO FUEL IT CAN USE!

KINETIC (or "MOVING") ENERGY

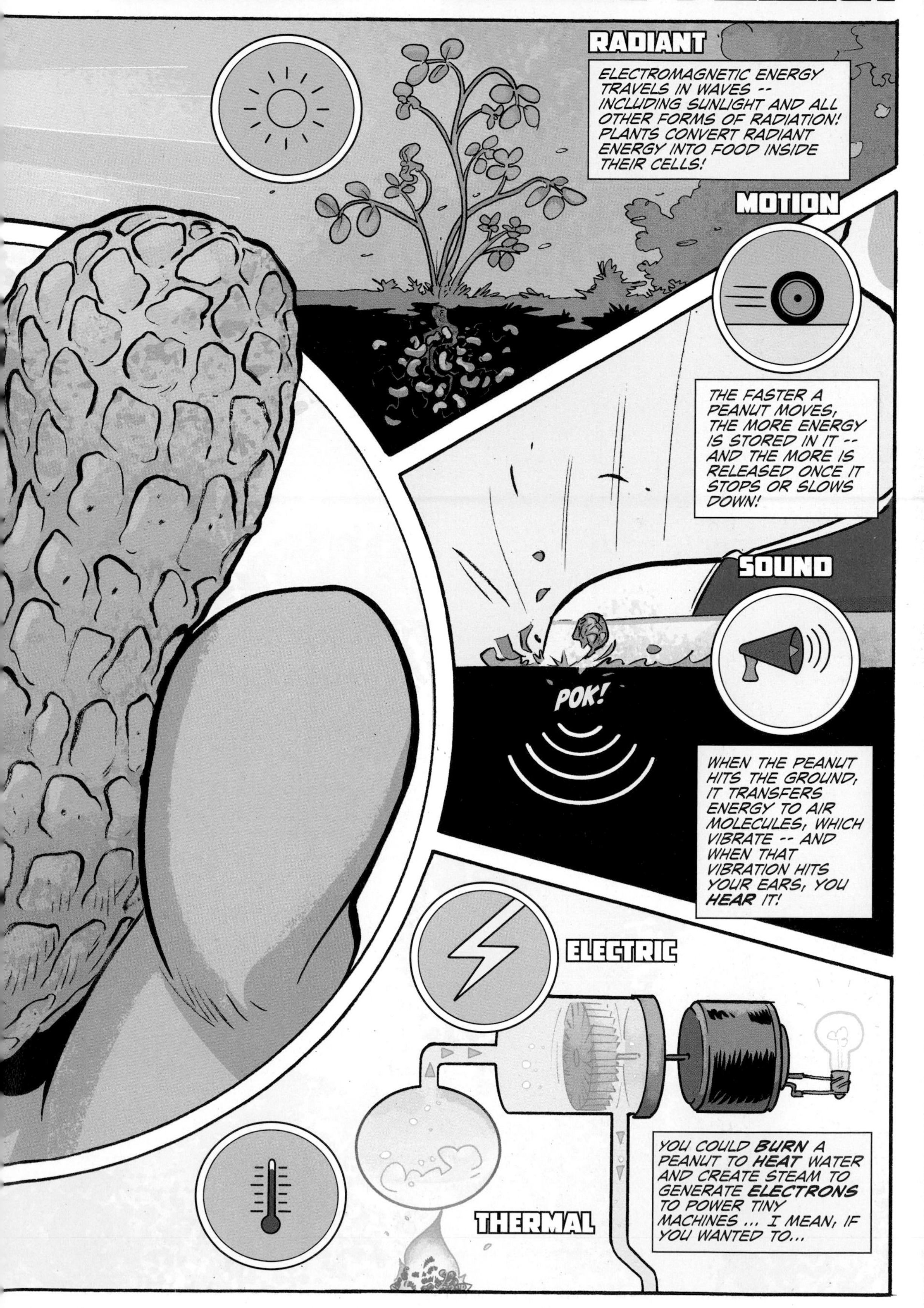

IN FACT, IF YOU REALLY WANTED TO, YOU COULD MEASURE ANY KIND OF WORK BY THE AMOUNT OF PEANUT POWER YOU'D NEED TO FUEL IT!
1 Peanut
1 PEANUT = 6 CALORIES
1 CALORIE = 4.184 JOULES
1 JOULES PER SECOND = 1 WATT

Running
(1 MILE) = 13 PEANUTS
(76 CALORIES)
(325 JOULES)
=
* CALCULATIONS ARE BASED ON A 100 POUND CHILD RUNNING A 10 MINUTE MILE.

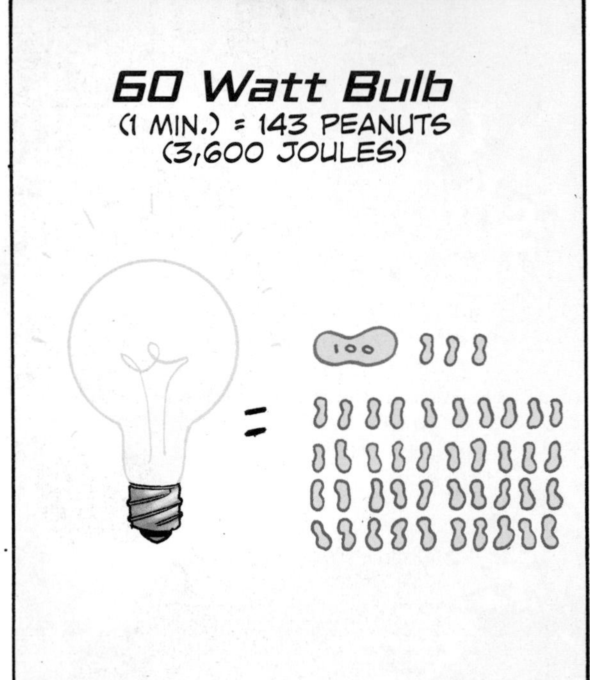
60 Watt Bulb
(1 MIN.) = 143 PEANUTS
(3,600 JOULES)
=
100

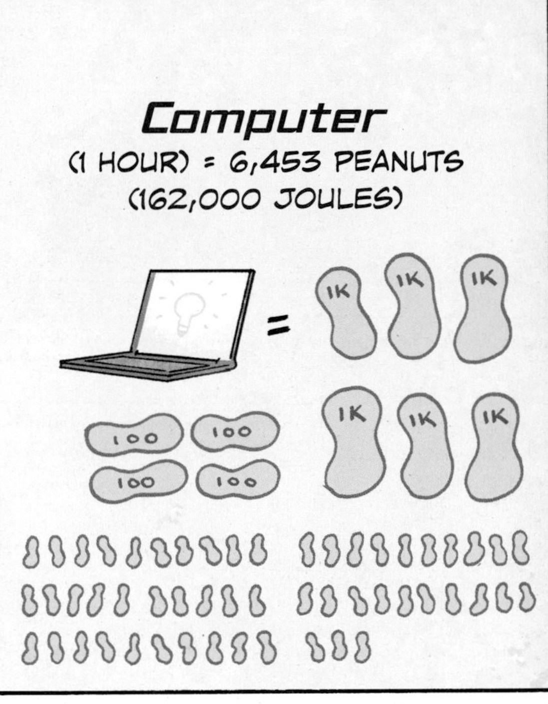
Computer
(1 HOUR) = 6,453 PEANUTS
(162,000 JOULES)
=
1K
100

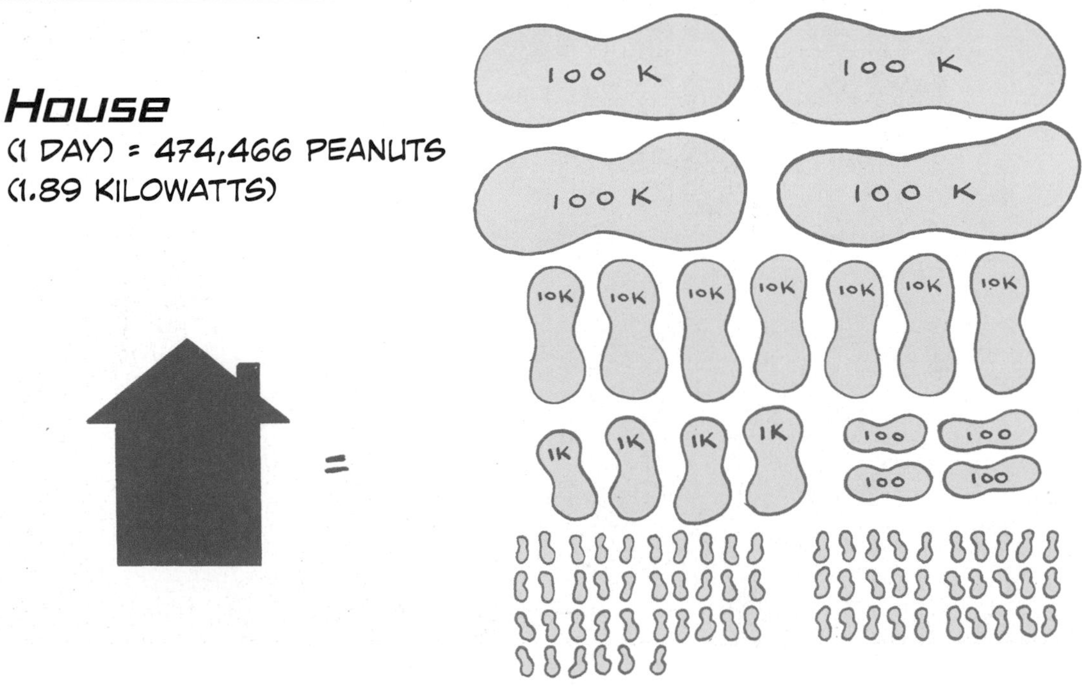
House
(1 DAY) = 474,466 PEANUTS
(1.89 KILOWATTS)
=
100 K
10K
1K
100

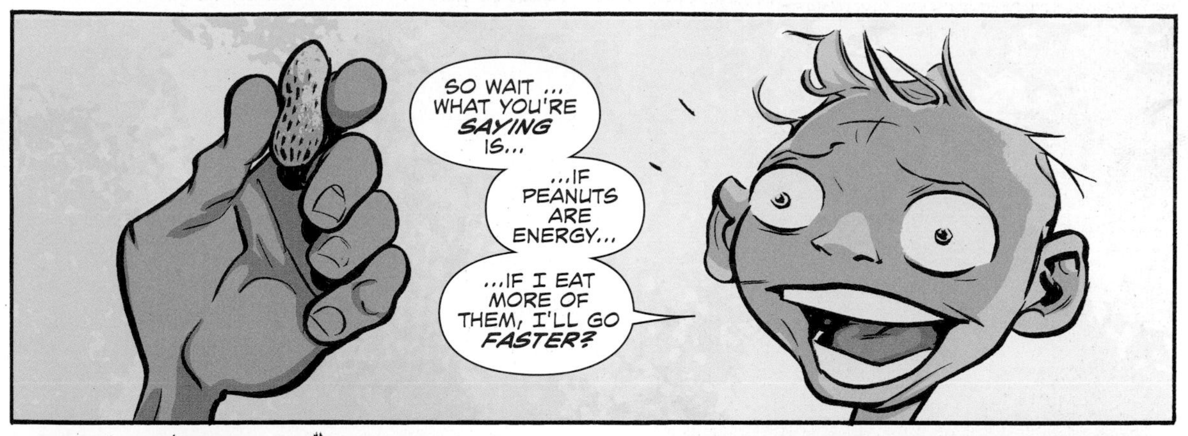
SO WAIT ... WHAT YOU'RE SAYING IS...
...IF PEANUTS ARE ENERGY...
...IF I EAT MORE OF THEM, I'LL GO FASTER?

AND WE MIGHT EVEN GET TO THE CITY IN SECONDS?!?
NOM NOM NOM NOM NOM
WELL... NO...
...JUST LIKE ANY OTHER KIND OF ENERGY, WHEN CHEMICAL ENERGY IS TRANSFERRED FROM ORGANISM TO ORGANISM, MOST OF IT IS DISSIPATED INTO THE ENVIRONMENT...

...SO ALL YOU'RE DOING BY STUFFING YOURSELF SO QUICKLY IS WASTING A LOT OF THAT ENERGY...
...AND PUTTING YOURSELF...
OOH... DON'T... FEEL SO GOOD...
ENERGY MAKES MY TUMMY HURT...

...INTO A FOOD COMA.
THUD

TUUUUCK... C'MON!
YOU'RE TOO HEAVY TO CARRY ALL THE WAY TO THE CITY!

CHAIR 'A' PALOOZA!
I NEED TO MULTIPLY MY STRENGTH...

...BUT I DON'T HAVE THE ENERGY TO...

NNNH...
WHAA...
WHOA!
WHEEEEEEEEE!!

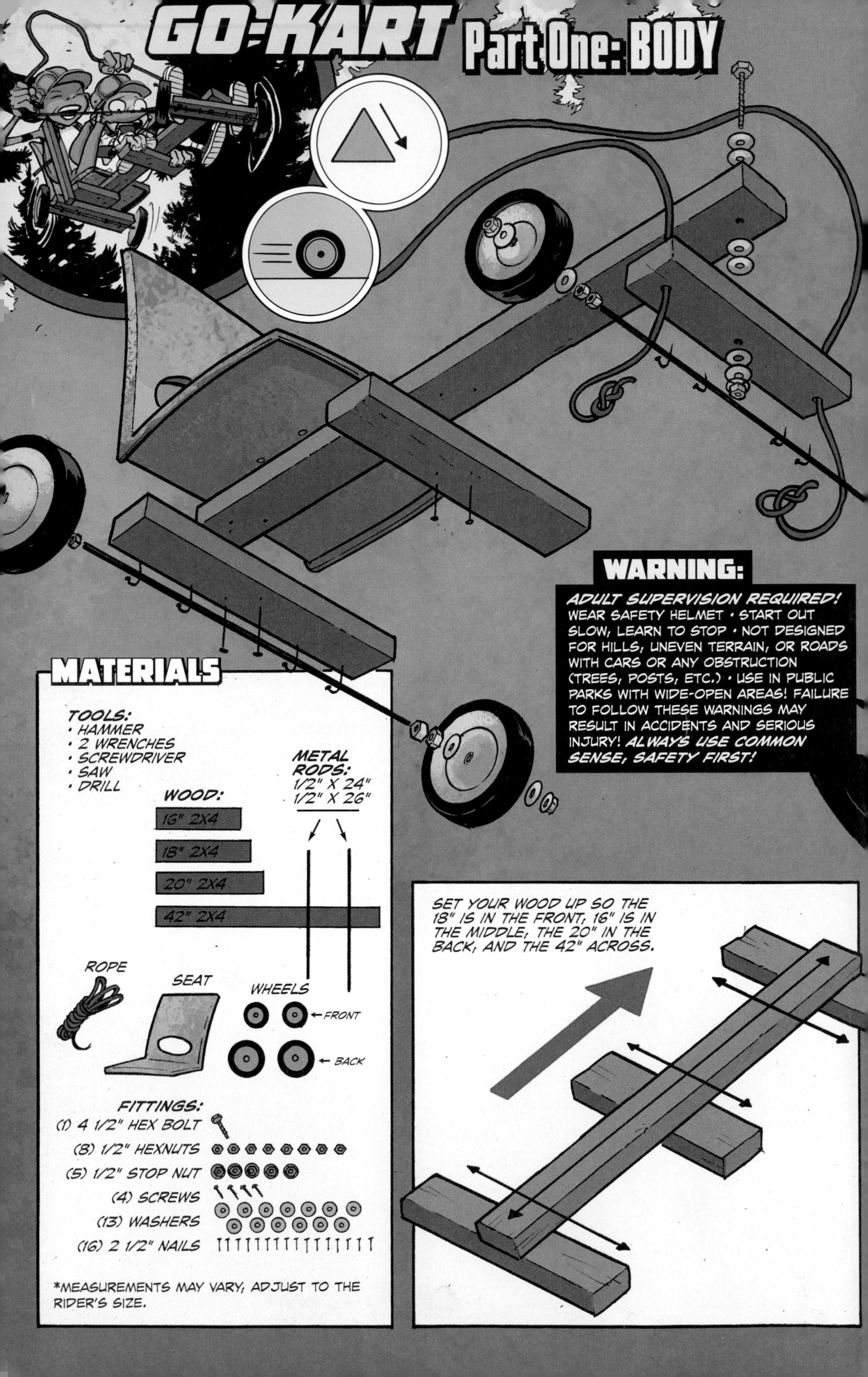
GO-KART Part One: BODY
WARNING:
ADULT SUPERVISION REQUIRED!
WEAR SAFETY HELMET • START OUT SLOW, LEARN TO STOP • NOT DESIGNED FOR HILLS, UNEVEN TERRAIN, OR ROADS WITH CARS OR ANY OBSTRUCTION (TREES, POSTS, ETC.) • USE IN PUBLIC PARKS WITH WIDE-OPEN AREAS! FAILURE TO FOLLOW THESE WARNINGS MAY RESULT IN ACCIDENTS AND SERIOUS INJURY! ALWAYS USE COMMON SENSE, SAFETY FIRST!
MATERIALS
TOOLS:
• HAMMER
• 2 WRENCHES
• SCREWDRIVER
• SAW
• DRILL
WOOD:
16" 2X4
18" 2X4
20" 2X4
42" 2X4
METAL RODS:
1/2" X 24"
1/2" X 26"
ROPE
SEAT
WHEELS
FRONT
BACK
FITTINGS:
(1) 4 1/2" HEX BOLT
(8) 1/2" HEXNUTS
(5) 1/2" STOP NUT
(4) SCREWS
(13) WASHERS
(16) 2 1/2" NAILS
*MEASUREMENTS MAY VARY; ADJUST TO THE RIDER'S SIZE.
SET YOUR WOOD UP SO THE 18" IS IN THE FRONT, 16" IS IN THE MIDDLE, THE 20" IN THE BACK, AND THE 42" ACROSS.

ATTACHING WHEELS TO BOTH AXLES:

THE BIGGER WHEELS ON THE BACK WITH THE 26" ROD. SMALL WHEELS IN THE FRONT WITH 24" ROD.

ON EACH SIDE THE ORDER IS:
STOP NUT, WASHER, WHEEL, HEX NUT. 2 HEX NUTS WILL LOCK EACH OTHER INTO PLACE.

USING TWO WRENCHES, FIRST LOCK THE STOP NUT. ALLOW ENOUGH ROOM FOR THE WHEEL TO SPIN. THEN LOCK THE OTHER SIDE USING THE TWO HEX NUTS.

ATTACHING AXLE RODS TO WOOD:

MEASURE STRAIGHT ACROSS THE WOOD. HAMMER 4 NAILS ALONG THE LINE HALFWAY INTO THE WOOD.
PUT WHEEL ON ROD AND BANG NAIL SO IT FOLDS OVER ROD, HOLDING IT IN PLACE.

ATTACHING WOOD TO FRAME:

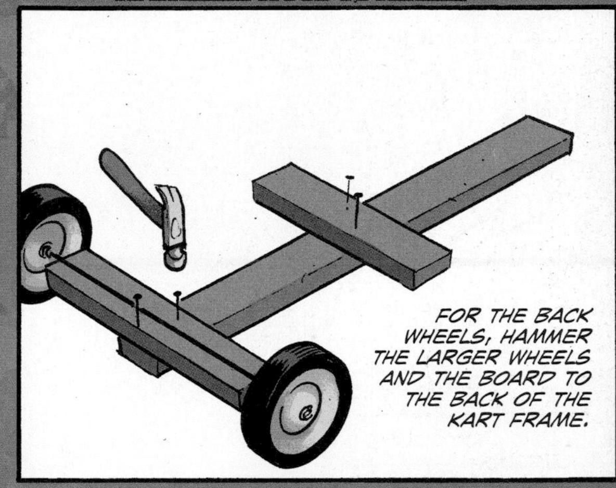

FOR THE BACK WHEELS, HAMMER THE LARGER WHEELS AND THE BOARD TO THE BACK OF THE KART FRAME.

FRONT STEERING:

USING A 5/8" BIT, HAND DRILL A HOLE THROUGH THE FRONT FRAME AND CENTER OF FRONT WHEELS.

ORDER: HEX BOLT, 2 WASHERS, WHEEL WOOD, 2 WASHERS, STOP NUT. TIGHTEN WITH WRENCH.

DRILL 2 HOLES ON EITHER SIDE OF THE FRONT WHEEL. TIE A KNOT. SLIDE OTHER END OF ROPE THROUGH, CREATING A REIN THAT IS BIG ENOUGH TO HOLD FROM THE SEAT.

ATTACHING THE SEAT:

SCREW IN SEAT TO WOODEN FRAME USING FOUR 1 1/2" WOOD SCREWS.

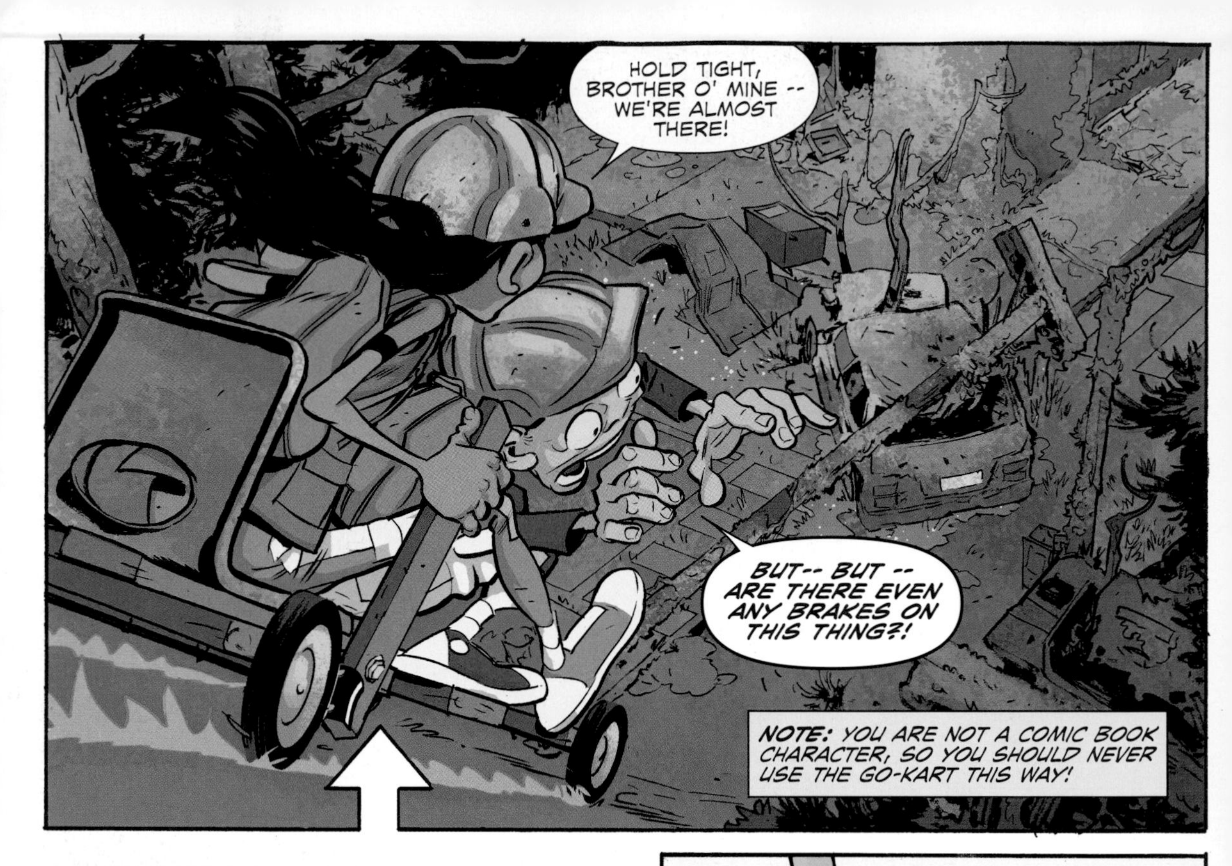

GO-KART Part Two: BRAKES

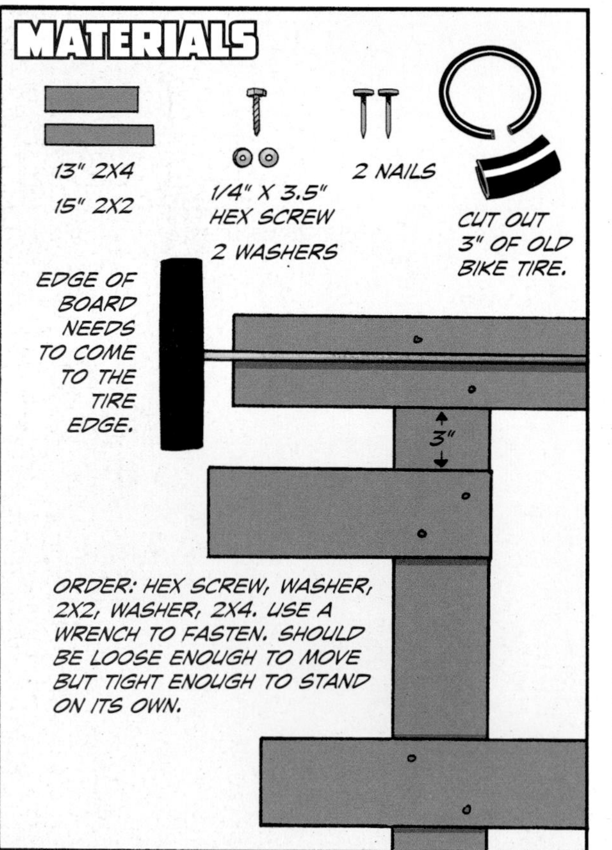

MATERIALS
13" 2X4
15" 2X2
1/4" X 3.5" HEX SCREW
2 WASHERS
2 NAILS
CUT OUT 3" OF OLD BIKE TIRE.
EDGE OF BOARD NEEDS TO COME TO THE TIRE EDGE.
3"
ORDER: HEX SCREW, WASHER, 2X2, WASHER, 2X4. USE A WRENCH TO FASTEN. SHOULD BE LOOSE ENOUGH TO MOVE BUT TIGHT ENOUGH TO STAND ON ITS OWN.

DEPENDING ON THE WHEEL HEIGHT, GIVE YOURSELF 1/2" TO 1" OFF THE MEASURE AND MARK WOOD.

DRILL 1/4" HOLE THROUGH 2X2. THEN SLIGHTLY SMALLER - 3/16" INTO THE 2X4 TO HELP SCREW IT IN.
ATTACH TIRE WITH 2 NAILS.

SKKRRSSHHHHHHH

THERE ARE EVEN BRAKES ON THIS THING.
WELL *GOOD.*

WE'RE ... WE'RE *HERE.*
BUT ... WHERE ARE THE *PEOPLE?*
IT'S SO *QUIET.*

LOOK! THE ROVER TRACKS! MOM AND DAD *WERE* HERE!

THIS WAY!

DINO ENERGY
BURNS
WITH
4U!
MOM!
MOM!
MOM!
DAD!
DAD!
DAD!

FORGET MOM AND DAD ... WHERE IS *ANYBODY?*
FORGET MOM AND DAD?!?!?
I DON'T MEAN IT LIKE *THAT,* BUT...
...DID DINO'S *BIG BOOM* WIPE OUT EVERYBODY ON EARTH BUT US?

CELINE! *LOOK!*

GONE ... *GONE!*
MOM! DAD!
NOT EVEN ANY FOOTPRINTS ... THEY JUST VANISHED...

MAYBE THEY DIDN'T GO... FAR...
LET'S ... WAIT HERE AND SEE IF THEY COME BACK...

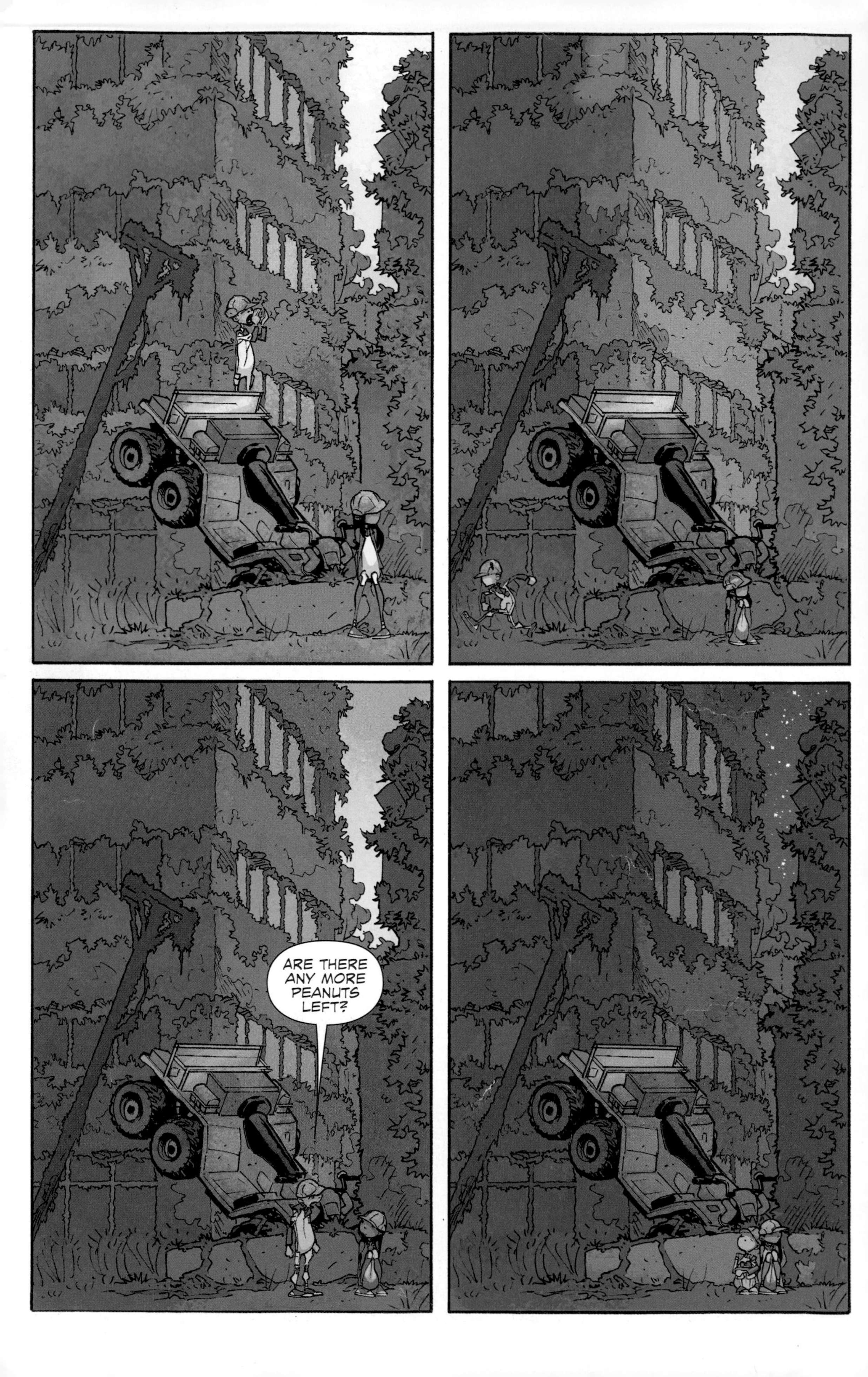
ARE THERE ANY MORE PEANUTS LEFT?

HEY. HEY, TUCK.
SNOR ... WHA...?

TUCK. I THINK...
WELL, IF MOM AND DAD WERE HERE, THEY AREN'T ANYMORE.
WE'RE ON OUR OWN ... MAYBE FOR A WHILE.

3
7
8
OKAY...
WE KNOW THERE'S FRESH WATER, PLUS THESE LOOK LIKE WILD POTATOES...

...WE'VE GOT FOOD AND WATER, SO WE NEED SHELTER!
THE TUCKSTER IS ON IT!
I TOO POSSESS INCREDIBLE ENERGY-KNOWING-THINGS!
TREMBLE IN SOME AWE FROM WHAT WILL BECOME FORT AWESOME!

UH... I APPRECIATE THE THOUGHT AND EVERYTHING, BUT... I'M JUST GONNA GO TRY AND GATHER SOME WOOD FOR A LONGER-LASTING STRUCTURE...
PFF! SURE, GO BREAK YOUR BACK, LUMBERJANE. I'LL HAVE A SHELTER UP IN NO TIME!

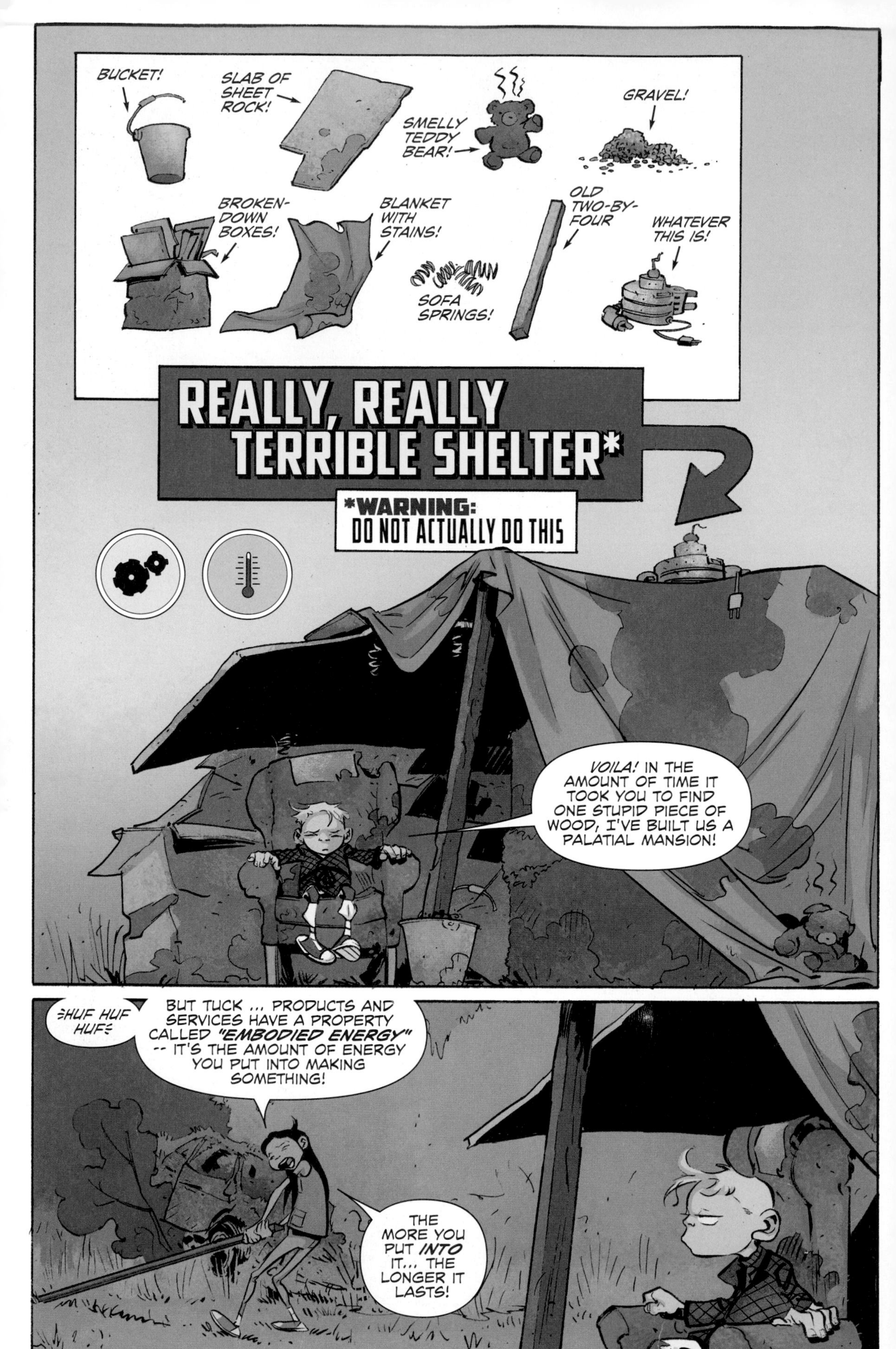
BUCKET!
SLAB OF SHEET ROCK!
SMELLY TEDDY BEAR!
GRAVEL!
BROKEN-DOWN BOXES!
BLANKET WITH STAINS!
SOFA SPRINGS!
OLD TWO-BY-FOUR
WHATEVER THIS IS!
REALLY, REALLY TERRIBLE SHELTER*
*WARNING: DO NOT ACTUALLY DO THIS
VOILA! IN THE AMOUNT OF TIME IT TOOK YOU TO FIND ONE STUPID PIECE OF WOOD, I'VE BUILT US A PALATIAL MANSION!
HUF HUF HUF
BUT TUCK ... PRODUCTS AND SERVICES HAVE A PROPERTY CALLED "EMBODIED ENERGY" -- IT'S THE AMOUNT OF ENERGY YOU PUT INTO MAKING SOMETHING!
THE MORE YOU PUT INTO IT... THE LONGER IT LASTS!

THAT'S NOT TRUE, CELINE!
MOM SAYS THE MOST IMPORTANT INGREDIENT IN ANYTHING IS LOVE!

TAP

KRASSSHH

HAHAHAHAHAHAHAHAHAHAHAHAHAHA
OH ... OH, THAT MAY BE TRUE!
BECAUSE I REALLY LOVED THAT!

I'VE HAD ENOUGH!
BONK
HEY! DON'T DO THAT!

ALL YOU DO IS ACT LIKE YOU'RE BETTER THAN ME AND SMARTER THAN ME!
WELL YOU'RE NOT!
I NEVER SAID THAT!

DON'T GET MAD BECAUSE I ACTUALLY LISTENED TO NANNI'S DREAMSCHOOL CARTRIDGES WHILE WE WERE IN STASIS INSTEAD OF PLAYING STUPID ZOMBIE GAMES!
DAD SAID WE MIGHT NEED TO FEND FOR OURSELVES IN WHATEVER WORLD WE FOUND WHEN WE WOKE UP--

SHUT UP! DON'T CALL HIM THAT!
HE'S NOT YOUR REAL DAD! HE'S MINE!
YOU'RE NOT MY REAL SISTER!

TUCK...
WHERE ARE YOU GOING?!
AND I DON'T NEED YOUR HELP TO FIND HIM!

UP THERE! WHY SHOULD WE EVEN BUILD SHELTERS WHEN WE'RE SURROUNDED BY BUILDINGS?

BUT -- THESE ARE RUINS! THEY COULD BE DANGEROUS -- YOU SHOULDN'T GO IN THERE!
WOW, AND IF I CARED WHAT YOU THOUGHT ABOUT ANYTHING, THAT MIGHT REALLY BOTHER ME!
GOODBYE, CELINE!

BUT...
I PROMISED MOM...
...TO PROTECT YOU...

119
SNFF
SNFFFL

MOM... DAD...
YOU'LL BE ABLE TO SEE THIS...

...AND COME BACK HERE...
...AND SAVE US...

PEANUTS

3

WUBOOOM

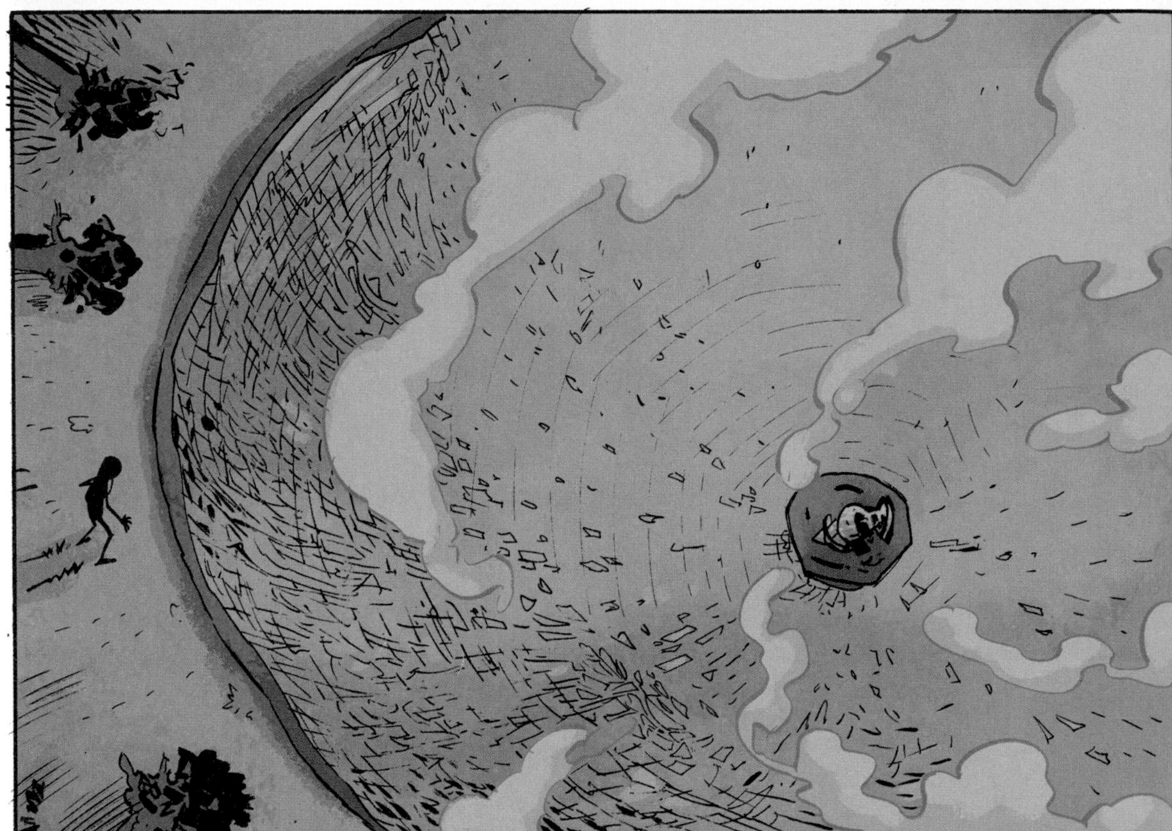

"A *SPACE* MIRROR?"

SERIOUSLY?
SERIOUSLY.
THE BLANKET TERM FOR THESE KINDS OF EFFORTS IS "GEO-ENGINEERING" --
-- IF WE CAN'T CHANGE PEOPLE'S BEHAVIOR, THEN WE HAVE TO CHANGE THE EARTH.
ON PURPOSE, THIS TIME.
RIGHT.

POLLUTION FROM THE BURNING OF FOSSIL FUELS CAUSES AN INCREASED "GREENHOUSE EFFECT"...

...TRAPPING HEAT IN THE ATMOSPHERE, WARMING THE WHOLE PLANET.

DINO ENERGY HAS NO INTEREST IN REDUCING CUSTOMERS' USE OF THEIR PRODUCTS. INSTEAD THEY'VE HIRED YOUR FATHER AND I TO TEST *OTHER* SOLUTIONS.

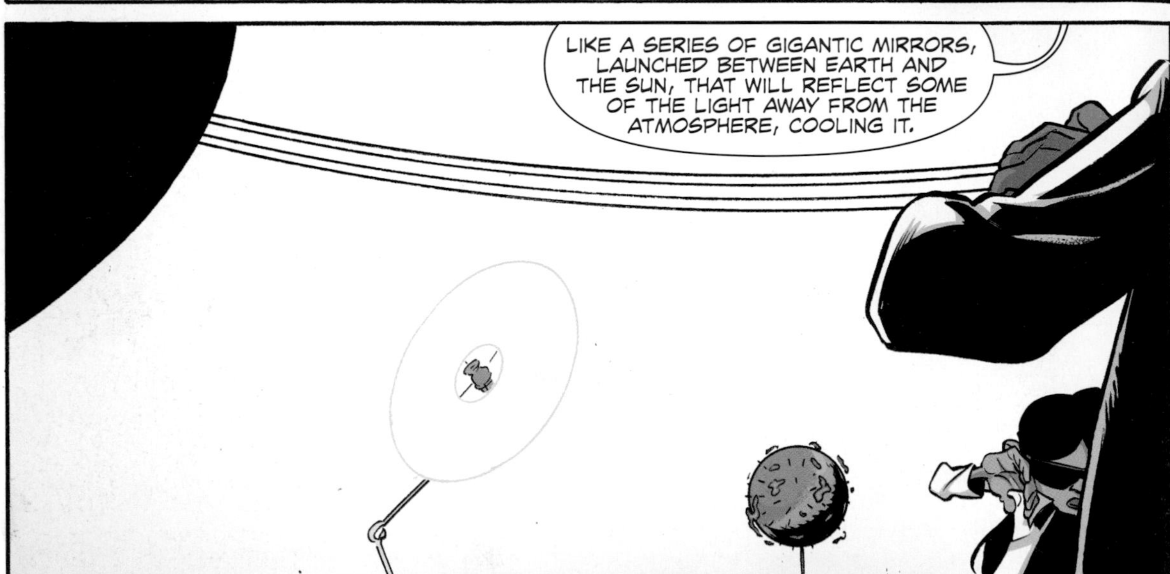
LIKE A SERIES OF GIGANTIC MIRRORS, LAUNCHED BETWEEN EARTH AND THE SUN, THAT WILL REFLECT SOME OF THE LIGHT AWAY FROM THE ATMOSPHERE, COOLING IT.

THEORETICALLY.

I DUNNO, MOM.
'SOUNDS LIKE SOMETHING OUT OF A *CARTOON.*
IS IT REALLY GONNA *WORK?*

WE BETTER HOPE SO.
BECAUSE IF IT DOESN'T...

"...DINO'S *NEXT* PLAN IS TO NUKE A BUNCH OF VOLCANOES ON *PURPOSE.*"
CAREFUL... *CAREFUL...*

KLUNK

LIVING LARGE ON SOLAR
The principles of solar architecture have been known since ancient times. We can make very comfortable housing that requires very little energy to heat or cool if we follow simple rules:
WINDOWS FACING SOUTH ALLOW SUNLIGHT TO ENTER -- THE WALL INSIDE THE WINDOWS TRAPS THE HEAT, SO MAKE IT WITH CONCRETE OR WATER-FILLED DRUMS!
WARM AIR ENTERS FROM THE TOP OF THAT WALL AND COOLS AS IT LOWERS TO THE FLOOR. IT GOES THROUGH THE BOTTOM VENT INTO THE "SUN ROOM" TO BE WARMED UP AGAIN!
THE WHOLE HOUSE IS VERY WELL-INSULATED WITH NO HEAT-LEAKY WINDOWS ON THE NORTH SIDE.

VEGGIE BOX
(4) 4FT 2X6
(4) 2FT 2X6
(4) 16" 4X4
WEED CLOTH
(16) 1" #8 WOOD SCREWS & (32) 3 1/2" #14 WOOD SCREWS
RAKE 2X4 AREA
BUILD BOX
A surprising amount of food can be grown in a small number of veggie boxes. They are ideal for greens (lettuce and kale) but also for treats like strawberries and cherry tomatoes.
TAMP POST INTO GROUND, STABILIZING GARDEN BOX.
STAPLE WEED CLOTH TO BOTTOM OF BOX
ADD DIRT -- FILL TO THE TOP.
COMPOST PILE
ALTERNATE LAYERS OF GREEN BIOMASS (KITCHEN SCRAPS, GREEN LEAVES, GRASS, OR FLOWER CLIPPINGS) AND BROWN BIOMASS (DRY LEAVES, STRAW, SHREDDED NEWSPAPER). BREAK DOWN WITH THE HELP OF BUGS, WORMS, AND BACTERIA INTO NUTRIENT-RICH COMPOST YOU CAN ADD TO SOIL TO FEED YOUR PLANTS!
BE SURE TO WATER YOUR COMPOST PILE AND TURN IT OVER WITH A RAKE OR HOE SO IT GETS AIR TOO -- BOTH ARE REQUIRED FOR THE COMPOSTING PROCESS!

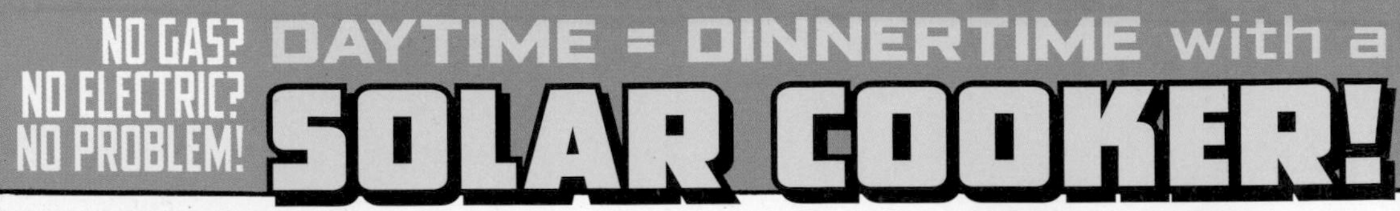
NO GAS? NO ELECTRIC? NO PROBLEM!
DAYTIME = DINNERTIME with a
SOLAR COOKER!

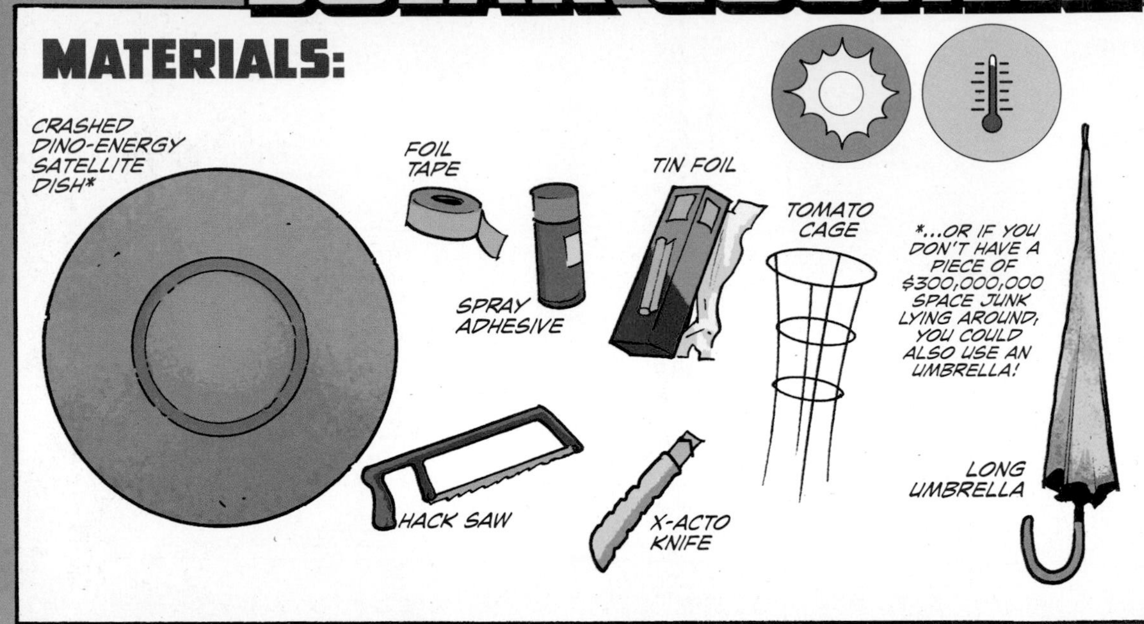
MATERIALS:
CRASHED DINO-ENERGY SATELLITE DISH*
FOIL TAPE
SPRAY ADHESIVE
TIN FOIL
TOMATO CAGE
*...OR IF YOU DON'T HAVE A PIECE OF $300,000,000 SPACE JUNK LYING AROUND, YOU COULD ALSO USE AN UMBRELLA!
HACK SAW
X-ACTO KNIFE
LONG UMBRELLA

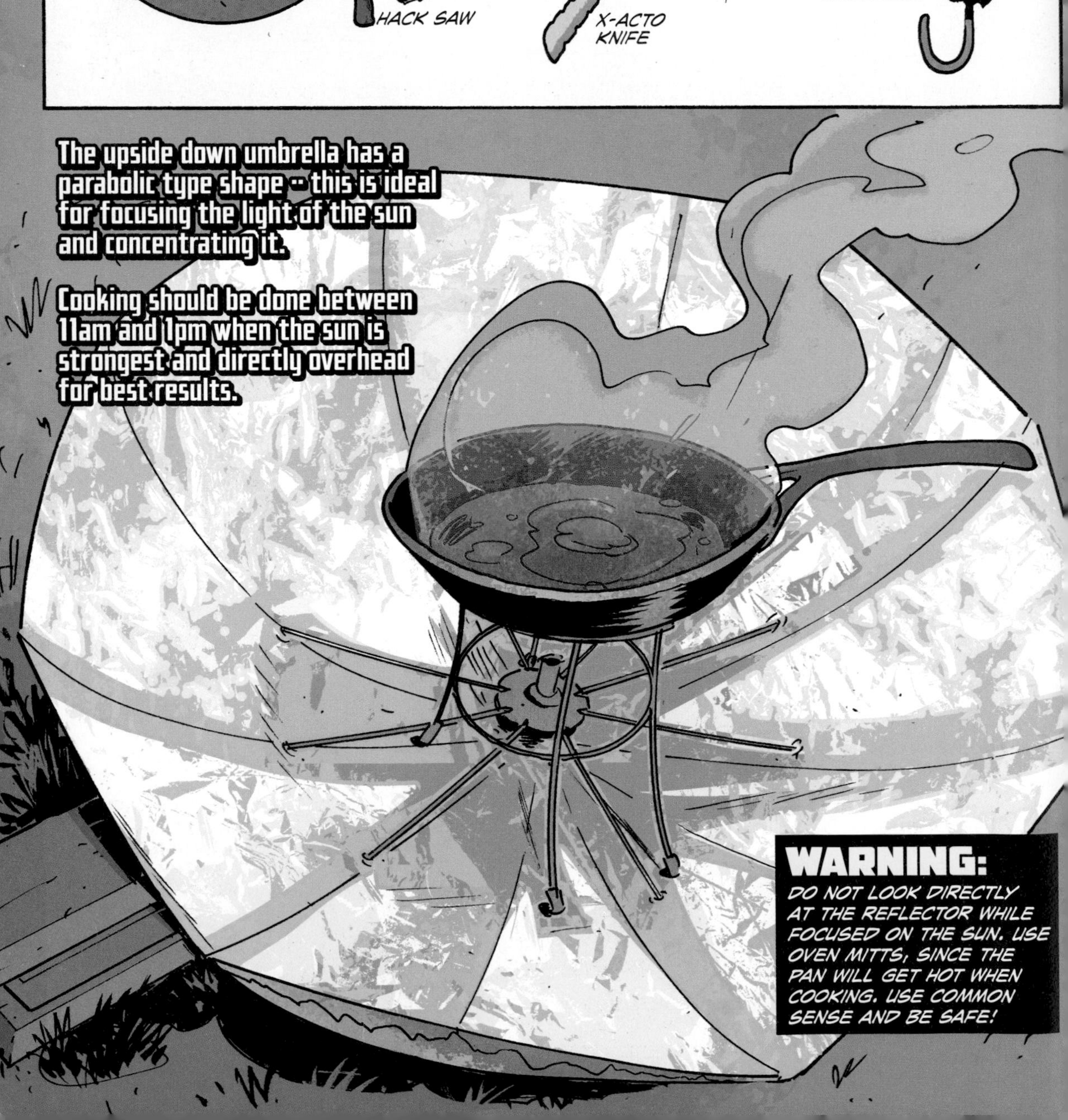
The upside down umbrella has a parabolic type shape -- this is ideal for focusing the light of the sun and concentrating it.
Cooking should be done between 11am and 1pm when the sun is strongest and directly overhead for best results.
WARNING:
DO NOT LOOK DIRECTLY AT THE REFLECTOR WHILE FOCUSED ON THE SUN. USE OVEN MITTS, SINCE THE PAN WILL GET HOT WHEN COOKING. USE COMMON SENSE AND BE SAFE!

USING A HACK SAW -- CUT HANDLE OFF.

SPRAY DULL SIDE OF TIN FOIL WITH GLUE, OR YOU CAN TAPE SIDES DOWN.

STICK GLUED SIDE DOWN TO UMBRELLA.

TRIM SIDES MAKING SURE THAT THE EDGES OVERLAP WITH EACH OTHER SO THE ENTIRE UMBRELLA IS COVERED IN FOIL.

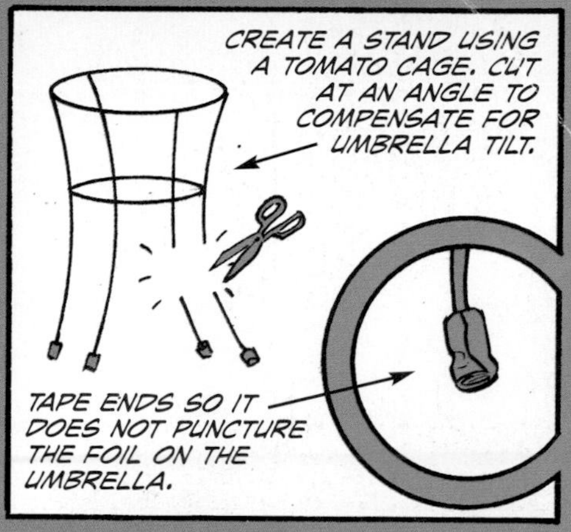

CREATE A STAND USING A TOMATO CAGE. CUT AT AN ANGLE TO COMPENSATE FOR UMBRELLA TILT.
TAPE ENDS SO IT DOES NOT PUNCTURE THE FOIL ON THE UMBRELLA.

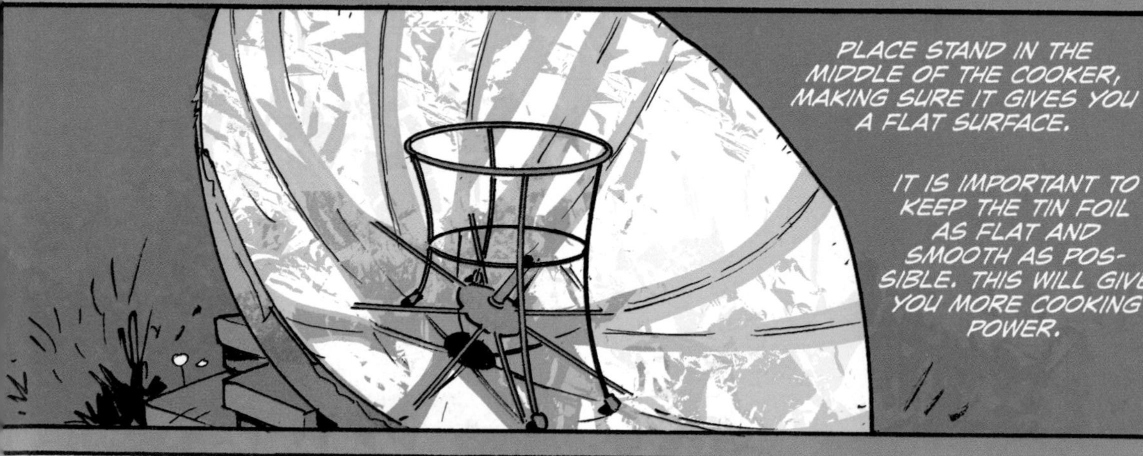

PLACE STAND IN THE MIDDLE OF THE COOKER, MAKING SURE IT GIVES YOU A FLAT SURFACE.
IT IS IMPORTANT TO KEEP THE TIN FOIL AS FLAT AND SMOOTH AS POSSIBLE. THIS WILL GIVE YOU MORE COOKING POWER.

CELINE'S VEGGIE SOLAR CHILI:

1 CUP OF CANNED BLACK BEANS
1 LARGE RIPE TOMATO DICED AND CRUSHED
1/4 ONION FINELY CHOPPED
1 EAR OF SWEET CORN KERNELS, COB REMOVED
1 GARLIC CLOVE MINCED
1 TABLESPOON OIL
1 TEASPOON CHILI POWDER
1/2 TEASPOON CUMIN
1/4 TEASPOON OREGANO
PINCH OF CAYENNE PEPPER
SALT AND PEPPER TO TASTE
CILANTRO

- IN A MEDIUM DARK POT, HEAT OIL WITH ONION AND GARLIC FOR 20 MIN.
- ADD BLACK BEANS, TOMATOES, CORN, CHILI POWDER, CUMIN, OREGANO, CAYENNE PEPPER, AND SALT AND PEPPER. COOK WITH LID FOR 1 1/2 HOURS. IT SLOW COOKS AT 180-200°
- OPTIONAL: ADD CHEESE AND COOK UNCOVERED.

SOLAR S'MORES:

- MARSHMALLOWS
- CHOCOLATE
- GRAHAM CRACKERS

- IN A DARK DISH OR PLATE. HEAT MARSHMALLOW FOR 30 MIN. PLACE CHOCOLATE ON GRAHAM CRACKER, HEAT FOR 10 MINUTES OR UNTIL MELTED. SMUSH TOGETHER AND ENJOY!

TUCK?
≈HFF≈
TUUUUUUCK?
≈HFF≈
I COME IN PEACE!
≈HFF≈
AND BEARING GIFTS!
TASTY GIF--

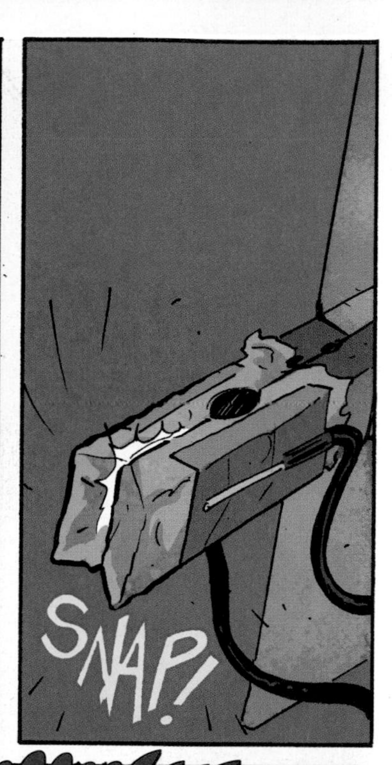
SNAP!

ARROOOOOOOOOOOGGHHHHAAHHH
RIP
EEYYAAGGHH!

TRIP WIRE SECURITY ALARM!

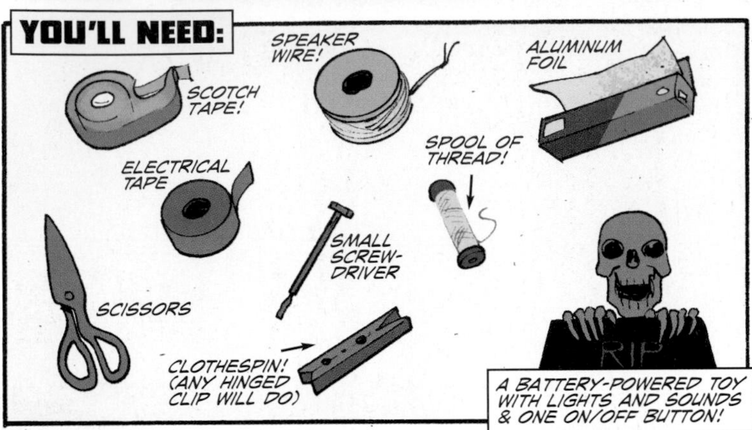

YOU'LL NEED:
SCOTCH TAPE!
SPEAKER WIRE!
ALUMINUM FOIL
ELECTRICAL TAPE
SPOOL OF THREAD!
SMALL SCREW-DRIVER
SCISSORS
CLOTHESPIN! (ANY HINGED CLIP WILL DO)
A BATTERY-POWERED TOY WITH LIGHTS AND SOUNDS & ONE ON/OFF BUTTON!

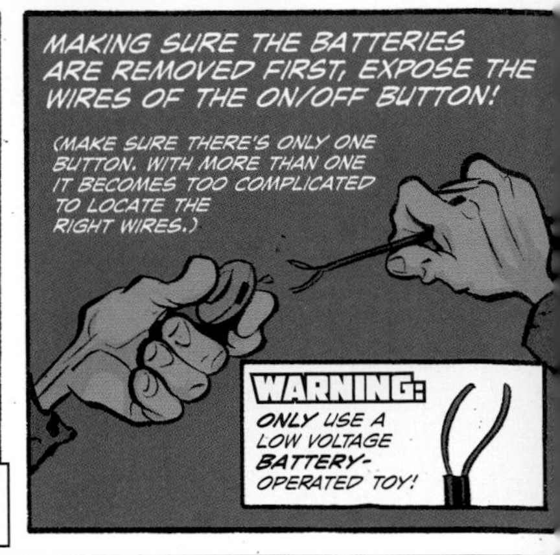

MAKING SURE THE BATTERIES ARE REMOVED FIRST, EXPOSE THE WIRES OF THE ON/OFF BUTTON!
(MAKE SURE THERE'S ONLY ONE BUTTON. WITH MORE THAN ONE IT BECOMES TOO COMPLICATED TO LOCATE THE RIGHT WIRES.)
WARNING: ONLY USE A LOW VOLTAGE BATTERY-OPERATED TOY!

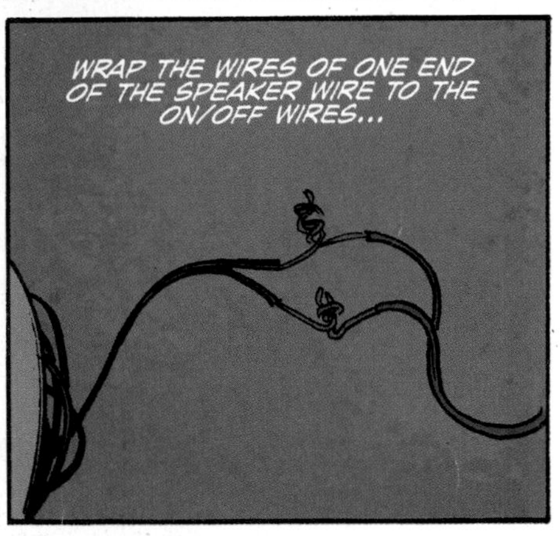

WRAP THE WIRES OF ONE END OF THE SPEAKER WIRE TO THE ON/OFF WIRES...

...AND TAPE THEM TOGETHER.

WRAP THE ENDS OF THE CLOTHESPIN WITH FOIL!

THEN SECURELY TAPE THE OTHER TWO ENDS OF THE SPEAKER WIRES UNDER THAT FOIL!

SECURE THE CLIP TO THE WALL IN A CONCEALED LOCATION...

...TAPE ONE END OF THE THREAD TO ONE SIDE OF A DOORWAY...

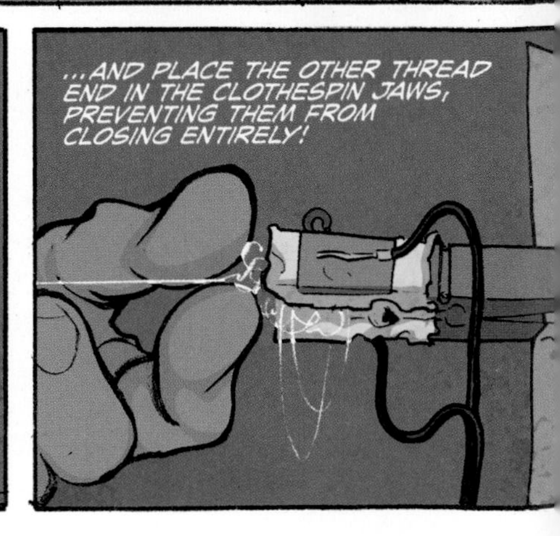

...AND PLACE THE OTHER THREAD END IN THE CLOTHESPIN JAWS, PREVENTING THEM FROM CLOSING ENTIRELY!

EVEN A THIN THREAD PREVENTS ELECTRICITY -- ELECTRONS -- FROM FLOWING THROUGH THE WIRES!
RIP

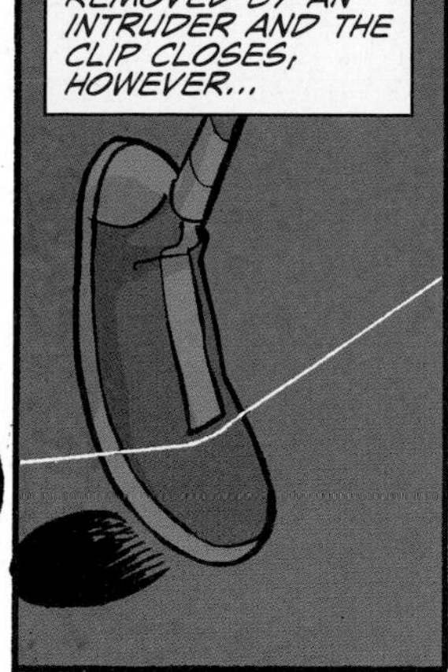
WHEN THE THREAD IS ACCIDENTALLY REMOVED BY AN INTRUDER AND THE CLIP CLOSES, HOWEVER...

...THE CIRCUIT IS COMPLETE, THE ENERGY FLOWS, AND YOUR NOISEMAKER COMES TO LIFE...
RIP

ARROOOOOOOOOGGAHAAAAHH
EEYYAAGGHH!

HA! NICE TRY, SNEAKY PETE!

YOUR NOSEY-NESS IS NO MATCH FOR MY NOISINESS!!!
GAAA! TUCK! GET OFF! IT'S ME! CELINE!

I WAS TRYING TO PATCH THINGS UP BETWEEN US BECAUSE YOU GOT ALL UPSET WHEN YOU THOUGHT I THOUGHT YOU WERE AN IDIOT...
ZZZIIPPPPPP

ZZZIIPPPPPP
...WHICH YOU'VE JUST TOTALLY PROVEN YOU TOTALLY ARE!!
YOU RUINED THE VEGETARIAN CHILI I MADE FOR US!

SSSH!
THAT'S NOT IMPORTANT RIGHT NOW!
WAIT FOR IT...

ZZZIIPPPPPP
AHHH! YOU HEAR THAT?
I THINK SO -- SOUNDS ALMOST LIKE ... BUGS BUZZING...

NO! NO NO NO NO NO...
EVER SINCE I STARTED SIGNALING MOM AND DAD WITH *MORSE CODE*--
--THREE SHORT, THEN THREE LONG, THEN THREE SHORT FLASHES, FOR "S.O.S."--
--I'VE BEEN HEARING *THAT*--AND SEEING FLASHES OF *MOVEMENT*--OUT OF THE CORNER OF MY EYE--ALL AROUND ME!
A B C D E F G H I J K L M N O P Q R S
T U V W X Y Z
1 2 3 4 5 6 7 8 9 0

SEE, *THIS* IS WHY WE HAVE TO BURY THE HATCHET AND STICK TOGETHER.
ZZZIIPPPPP
ON YOUR OWN YOU'VE GONE TOTALLY *PARANOID!*

THERE'S ONLY ONE WAY *UP* HERE, AND THAT'S *THIS* WAY!
WE WOULD'VE *SEEN* ANOTHER PERSON!

WELL... WHEN YOU PUT IT THAT WAY...
...MAYBE YOU'RE RIGHT...

...IT COULD BE NOTHING.

TUCK!
AAAAAGGGHHH!!

COME BACK HERE!
THERE'S NOWHERE TO GO BUT--

NO!!

TUCK! TUCK! OH, NO! I CAN'T LOSE YOU!
NOT WITHOUT SAYING I'M...

WHOA.

ZIP-LINES!
RAD.

ZZIIPPPP

HANG ON TUCK! I'M COMING!
I'M--
I'M TERRIFIED!
ZZZIIPPPPP
ZZZIIPPPP
I'M ABSOLUTELY, POSITIVELY TERRIFIED!
WHUFF
OKAY.
CLICK
OKAY...

ZZZIIPPPPP
I THINK I COULD GET THE HANG OF--
UH-OH.
CLINK
AAAHHHHHHHHH--
CRNNNCH

CELINE!

--HUH?

CELINE!! DON'T WORRY, I'LL FIND Y--
FORGET HER. SHE IS WITH THE STORMBREAKERS NOW.
THE -- HUH?

THE ANCIENT ENEMIES OF OUR TRIBE.
YOU POSSESS THE POWER OF THE LIGHT.
WE HEARD YOU BRING OUT A SCREAM FROM NOWHERE.

YOU CAUSED THE STAR TO FALL FROM THE SKY.
YOU WILL TEACH WE ORPHANS HOW TO DO THESE THINGS. WE WILL USE THEM TO SMITE THOSE-WHO-JUDGE--
WHOA, HEY NOW YOU GUYS, I THINK WE GOT SOME KIND OF MISUNDERSTA--
I CAN'T--

--OR HE-WHO-BURNS WILL USE YOU FOR KINDLING.
GULP!

4

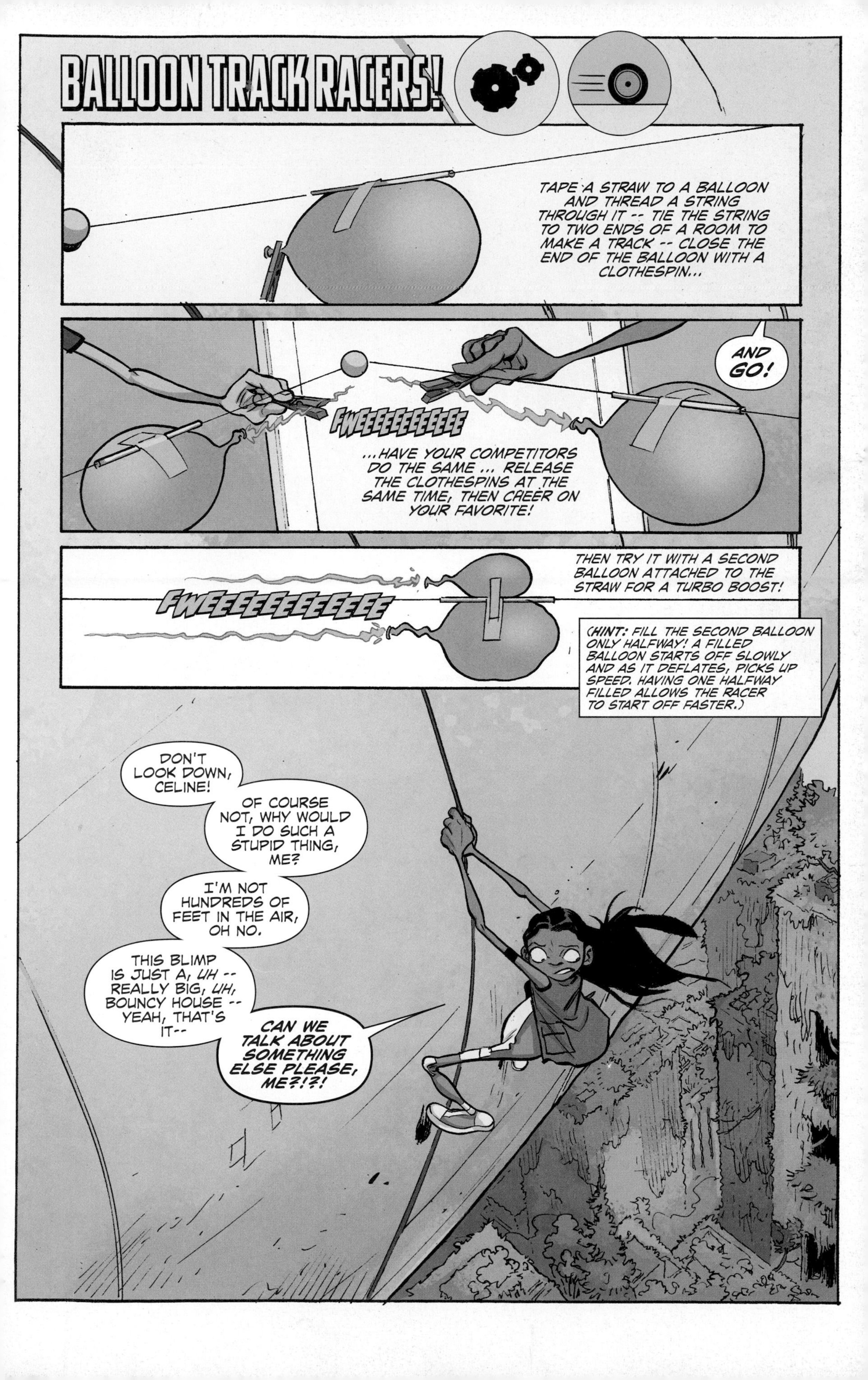
BALLOON TRACK RACERS!
TAPE A STRAW TO A BALLOON AND THREAD A STRING THROUGH IT -- TIE THE STRING TO TWO ENDS OF A ROOM TO MAKE A TRACK -- CLOSE THE END OF THE BALLOON WITH A CLOTHESPIN...
AND GO!
FWEEEEEEEEEE
...HAVE YOUR COMPETITORS DO THE SAME ... RELEASE THE CLOTHESPINS AT THE SAME TIME, THEN CHEER ON YOUR FAVORITE!
THEN TRY IT WITH A SECOND BALLOON ATTACHED TO THE STRAW FOR A TURBO BOOST!
FWEEEEEEEEEEE
(HINT: FILL THE SECOND BALLOON ONLY HALFWAY! A FILLED BALLOON STARTS OFF SLOWLY AND AS IT DEFLATES, PICKS UP SPEED. HAVING ONE HALFWAY FILLED ALLOWS THE RACER TO START OFF FASTER.)
DON'T LOOK DOWN, CELINE!
OF COURSE NOT, WHY WOULD I DO SUCH A STUPID THING, ME?
I'M NOT HUNDREDS OF FEET IN THE AIR, OH NO.
THIS BLIMP IS JUST A, UH -- REALLY BIG, UH, BOUNCY HOUSE -- YEAH, THAT'S IT--
CAN WE TALK ABOUT SOMETHING ELSE PLEASE, ME?!?!

YAAAAH!!
GOT YOU, FILTHY ORPHAN!

OVER THE SIDE WITH HER, BEFORE HER IGNORANCE INFECTS THE WHOLE SHIP!!!
WAIT! NO! I'M NO "ORPHAN!"
MY PARENTS ARE JUST MISSING --
THEY'RE SCIENTISTS, HAVE YOU SEEN THEM!?
HMMM ... SHE HAS SLIGHTLY BETTER HYGIENE THAN THE AVERAGE ORPHAN ... AND LESS BODY ART...

YOU HAVE PARENTS, YOU SAY? AND THEY'RE SCIENTISTS, YOU SAY?
YES -- THEY USED TO BE TOP RESEARCHERS FOR DINOSAUR ENERGY!
YOU DON'T SAY!
I -- I DO SAY.
I MEAN, I JUST SAID IT.

WHY, THAT'S WHAT WE USED TO BE -- OR RATHER, OUR ANCESTORS WERE!
WE ARE THE
STORMBREAKERS.

"AFTER DINO-E'S ATTEMPT TO GEO-ENGINEER THE CLIMATE WITH VOLCANOES AND MIRRORS FAILED, THEY SET OUR GREAT-GREAT-GREAT-GRANDPARENTS OFF IN THESE GREAT AIRSHIPS.
"...WE WERE TO SEED THE ATMOSPHERE WITH SULFATES TO DEFLECT SUNLIGHT AWAY FROM EARTH!

"WE WERE TRAPPED UP HERE WHILE THE RESOURCE WARS WERE WAGED...

"...AND NOW, IN THIS QUIET AFTERMATH, WE ARE THE KEEPERS OF ALL OF MANKIND'S SCIENTIFIC KNOWLEDGE...WAITING FOR THE EMERGENCE OF A CIVILIZATION WHICH MAY APPRECIATE IT!

"OUR INSTRUMENTS SPOTTED A FALLING SATELLITE NOT LONG AGO, AND WE HOPED IT MIGHT CONTAIN VALUABLE TECHNOLOGY WE COULD SALVAGE--"

OH, THE DINO-E SPACE MIRROR? YEAH, I FOUND THAT. IT'S BASICALLY SEVEN MILLION YEARS OF BAD LUCK AT THE BOTTOM OF A CRATER, NOW.
IS THAT SO? AH, WELL, IT WAS WORTH A TRY.
HELMSMEN! BRING US BACK UP TO SEVEN THOUSAND FEE--
WAIT, MA'AM!!

THOSE SNEAKY SCAVENGERS ARE TRYING TO PLUNDER OUR WIND FARM AGAIN!
THEY HAVE NO IDEA HOW TO USE IT, BUT THEM PICKING THROUGH IT LIKE MONKEYS WILL DAMAGE IT QUITE A BIT!

UGH! WORSE THAN COCKROACHES--
EINSTEIN TESLA!
YES, MOM! I MEAN MA'AM!
WAIT -- THOSE TRIBESPEOPLE HAVE GOTTA BE THE SAME ONES WHO CAPTURED MY BROTHER!
DON'T HURT THEM -- YOU MIGHT HIT TUCKER BY ACCIDENT!

"HURT" THEM? OH, YOU DARLING, SILLY LITTLE GIRL!
WE WOULD NEVER STOOP TO THE ORPHANS' LEVEL BY HURTING THEM...
WHEW! WELL, THAT'S GOOD.
EINSTEIN...

...REMIND THEM WHY THEY FEAR US.

RRRRMMMMMMMMMMBBBBBBBBBB
THE ONES WHO JUDGE HAVE UNLEASHED THE THUNDER!!
LEAVE THE *PRETTY PINWHEELS* FOR ANOTHER TIME -- WE HAVE THE REST OF OUR SALVAGE!

AND OUR CAPTIVE!
SILENCE, STUPID DUMB BABY WHO IS STUPID AND DUMB!
MMMF MMMFFF!

OOOOH HOW I HATE THE ONES WHO JUDGE -- IN THEIR FAT SHIPS THAT LOOK LIKE *GIANT ZITS!*
IF ONLY WE HAD OUR *STOMP-ROCKETS,* WE COULD POP YOU -- WE COULD POP YOU *GOOD,* JUDGY FLOATING ZITS!

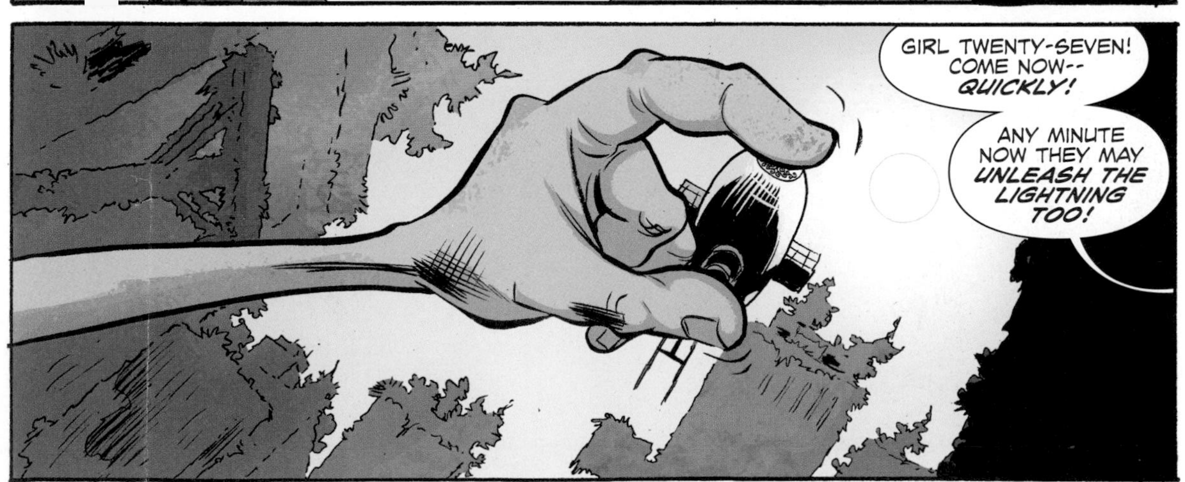
GIRL TWENTY-SEVEN! COME NOW-- *QUICKLY!*
ANY MINUTE NOW THEY MAY *UNLEASH THE LIGHTNING TOO!*

RRRMMMMMMMMBBBBBBBBB
TO THE FIRE BOATS!
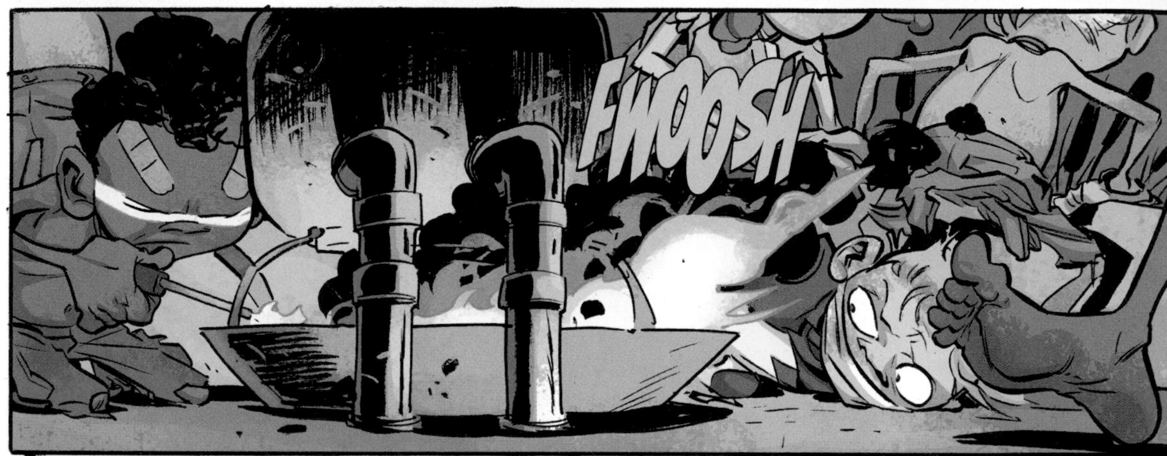
FWOOSH

BBBBUBBBBBUBBBBB
PUTPUTPUTPUTPUTPUT

PUTPUTPUTPUTPUTPUT
HA HA HA HA! LOOK AT THEM GO!

IGNORANT SCAVENGERS!
FOOLING THEM IS *LITERALLY* CHILD'S PLAY!
RRRRMMMMMMMMMMBBBBB

THUNDER DRUM

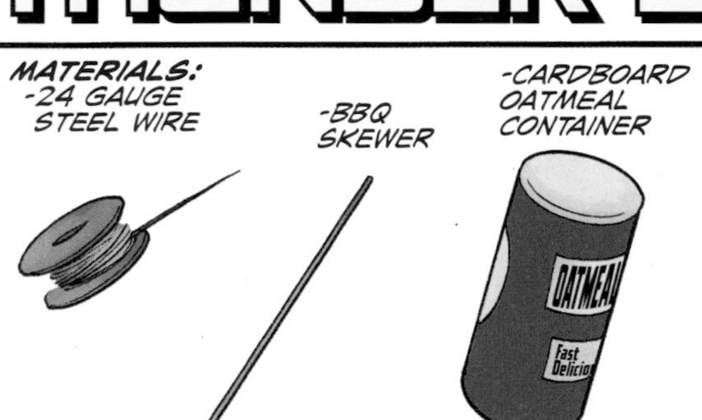

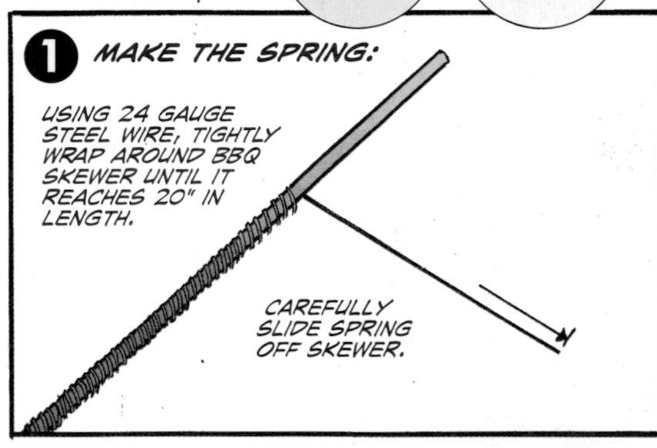

1 MAKE THE SPRING:
USING 24 GAUGE STEEL WIRE, TIGHTLY WRAP AROUND BBQ SKEWER UNTIL IT REACHES 20" IN LENGTH.
CAREFULLY SLIDE SPRING OFF SKEWER.

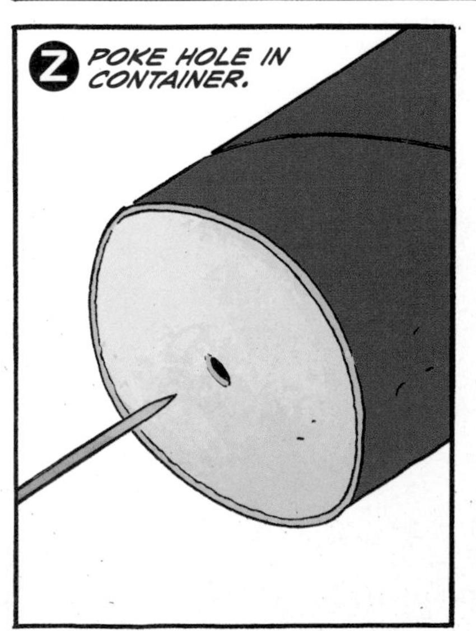

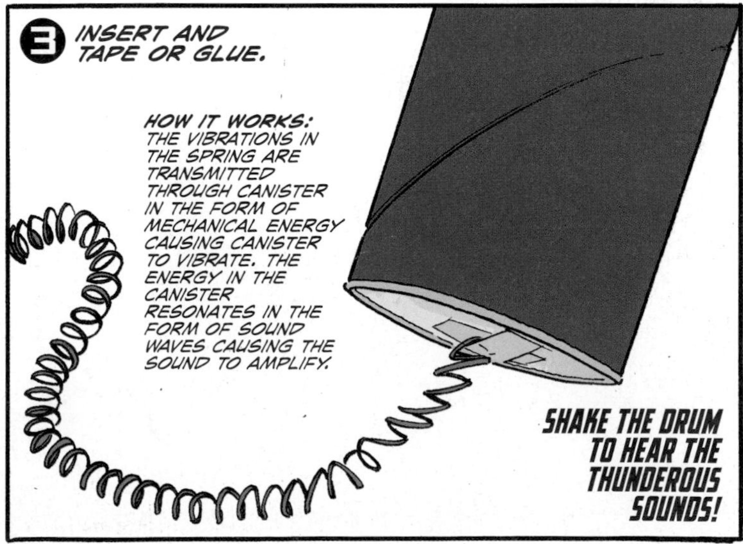

3 INSERT AND TAPE OR GLUE.
HOW IT WORKS: THE VIBRATIONS IN THE SPRING ARE TRANSMITTED THROUGH CANISTER IN THE FORM OF MECHANICAL ENERGY CAUSING CANISTER TO VIBRATE. THE ENERGY IN THE CANISTER RESONATES IN THE FORM OF SOUND WAVES CAUSING THE SOUND TO AMPLIFY.
SHAKE THE DRUM TO HEAR THE THUNDEROUS SOUNDS!

WHY ARE YOU LAUGHING AT THEM? OF COURSE THEY'RE IGNORANT, IF NOBODY'S TAUGHT THEM ANYTHING!
AND WHOSE FAULT IS THAT?
YOURS, IF YOU HAVE ALL THIS KNOWLEDGE AND WON'T SHARE IT!
WE TRIED SHARING IT! AND NONE OF IT STUCK!

WHAT DO THESE SCRIBBLES MEAN?
I HAVE NO IDEA!
FROM THE STORMBREAKERS

HEY! THAT ONE LOOKS LIKE A SIDEWAYS BUTT!

THEY'RE CALLING US SIDEWAYS BUTTS!
THAT OR OUR BUTTS ARE SIDEWAYS! ONE OF THE TWO!
WE MUST DESTROY THOSE WHO JUDGE!!

WELL, YOU DON'T KNOW WHY YOU FAILED. IF YOU JUST WENT DOWN THERE...
GASP!!!
DOWN? NO! NO, WE NEVER GO DOWN!

SO... YOU GUYS NEVER... LEAVE YOUR BALLOON?
AND TOUCH THE GROUND? NO! IT'S SWARMING WITH BEASTS AND DISEASES AND BANDITS AND COOTIES!

WE HAVE STAYED UP IN THE CLOUDS FOR FOUR GENERATIONS AS ONE, BIG, HAPPY FAMILY!
I LOST MY FAMILY, SO IT MUST BE NICE...

YOU HAVE PROVEN YOU'RE NOT LIKE THOSE IGNORANT ORPHANS, LITTLE GIRL -- YOU CAN JOIN US, IF YOU WISH!
MY SON, EINSTEIN TESLA, COULD USE A COMPANION!
HEWWO.
GAHHHH! WELL, UH... THAT'S... NOT-WEIRD AT ALL...
...BUT... I'M NOT SO SURE...

UHP! SHE DOESN'T WANT THE BENEFITS OF SAFETY, SECURITY, AND HOT SHOWERS!
GOOD LUCK! NICE LIFE!
WAIT! NO! NOT THAT EITHER!

EEK! I COULD REALLY USE TUCK AND HIS WAY WITH PEOPLE RIGHT NOW! I CAN'T GET THESE GUYS TO LISTEN TO ME!

"OH WHY OH WHY DID I EVER LET US GET SEPARATED?!"
PUTPUTPUTPUTPUTPUT

MIGHTY ORPHAN WARRIORS! YOU HAVE RETURNED WITH KINDLING?
WE HAVE, HE-WHO-BURNS!

EXCELLENT! THROW IT ON THE FIRE, THEN -- IT IS ALMOST OUT!
SQWEEK SQWEEK SQWEEK SQWEEK
Y-YESSIR!

BUT WE WERE UNABLE TO FIND ANY OF THE SACRED C'S AND D'S -- ONLY AA'S AND AAA'S!
BAH! YOU DISPLEASE ME!
SQWEEK SQWEEK SQWEEK SQWEEK
SQWEEK SQWEEK SQWEEK SQWEEK
HE'S -- HE'S GONNA MAKE THE FACE!

NO! WAIT, HE-WHO-BURNS! LOOK -- WE FOUND THIS ONE -- IN THE RUINS OF THE CITY!
HE ALSO POSSESSES THE SECRET OF THE MAKING-OF-LIGHT!
SHOW ME.
SQWEEK SQWEEK SQWEEK SQWEEK SQWEEK SQWEEK SQWEEK

SPUTTER! COUGH!
MAN, WHAT ARE YOU GUYS SO WORRIED ABOUT *LIGHT* FOR? THAT'S THE *LEAST* OF YOUR ENERGY PROBLEMS!

WHAT?!
WHAT DID YOU SAY?

YOU'RE *WASTING* ALL THIS ENERGY LOOKING FOR THE FUEL TO POWER THIS STUPID *FAN* -- THERE'S GOTTA BE A *BETTER* WAY OF DOING IT!
OOOH THE FACE
HE'S GONNA GET THE *FACE*

YOU DARE JUDGE MY LIFESTYLE CHOICES?!
AAAWWW SNAP THERE IT IS

OOHH
JUDGEY
SUPER-JUDGEY
JUDGEY
JUDGER McJUDGSON
SIR JUDGES-A-LOT OF JUDGESHIRE
HE'S GETTIN' JUDGEY WITH IT
WELCOME TO JUDGEY TOWN, POPULATION HIM.
WHAT? WHAT'D I SAY?

EVER SINCE THE ADULTS VANISHED, LEAVING US TO FEND FOR OURSELVES, WE ORPHANS HAVE OBEYED CERTAIN SACRED LAWS!
SUCH AS?

SUCH AS HE WHO SMELT IT --
-- VERILY, HE ALMOST ALWAYS IS THE ONE WHO HATH ALSO DEALT IT.
PEE-YOU!

THE PEOPLE, THEY ARE RUBBER.
I SAY TO OUR ENEMIES -- YOU ARE GLUE!
ANYTHING YOU SAY, THOSE WORDS BOUNCE OFF ME--
--AND STICK VERY MUCH TO YOU!
YEAH, I THINK I'VE HEARD THAT ONE BEFORE...

AND LAST BUT MOST IMPORTANTLY -- HE WHO DOES NOT PUT UP--
YEA, WE SAY UNTO HIM--

--HE MUST THEN VERILY SHUT UP!

PFFF! NO PROBLEM! LOOK: MY IMPROV FLASHLIGHT TOTALLY...
CLICK
CLICK

...UH...
...HAS DEAD BATTERIES, TOO... ALL THAT MORSE CODE... ULP!
CLICK
CLICK CLICK
CLICK CLICK

BEHOLD THE ASH-CLOCK, UPLANDER! OUR SACRED TIMEPIECE!
YOU HAVE UNTIL ONE END EMPTIES INTO THE OTHER TO FIND A POWER SOURCE FOR -- THE LIGHT.

OR YOU MAY BECOME KINDLING YOURSELF.
GULP!

GO!
OKAY, OKAY! I'M GOING! I'M GOING!

BATTERIES... OKAY, BATTERIES... BATTERIES...

GONE -- ALL GONE!
I'M GONNA RUN OUTTA TIME!

GAHH! NADA! AGAIN!
IF ONLY CELINE WAS HERE! OH WHY DID I MAKE HER MAD?
SHE COULD NOODLE HER WAY OUT OF THIS!

OH PLEASE OH PLEASE OH PLEASE --
-- SOMEBODY, SOMEWHERE --
-- SHOW ME A SIGN!

BONK

HAH! YOUR TIME IS *UP*, JUDGEY ONE!

AND WE *BOTH* KNOW YOU DID NOT HAVE ENOUGH TIME TO FIND ANY *BATTERIES* -- ORPHANS LONG BEFORE US PICKED THIS RUIN CLEAN.
ARE YOU READY TO ADMIT THAT THE ONLY REAL FUEL IS THAT WHICH *BURNS?!*

SUBMIT, UPLANDER! *SUBMIT* BEFORE THE *BURNI*--

CLICK!

OOOOOOOOOOOOOOOOOO
BY THE ETERNAL STERNO!!! HOW?!

YOU MAY BE ONE WHO BURNS, KID...
...BUT I'M ONE WHO *SPUDS!*

POTATO POWER!

MATERIALS:

6 ALLIGATOR CLIPS

1.5-3 V LED

6 GALVANIZED ZINC NAILS

6 NEW COPPER PENNIES

3 POTATOES (CUT IN HALF)

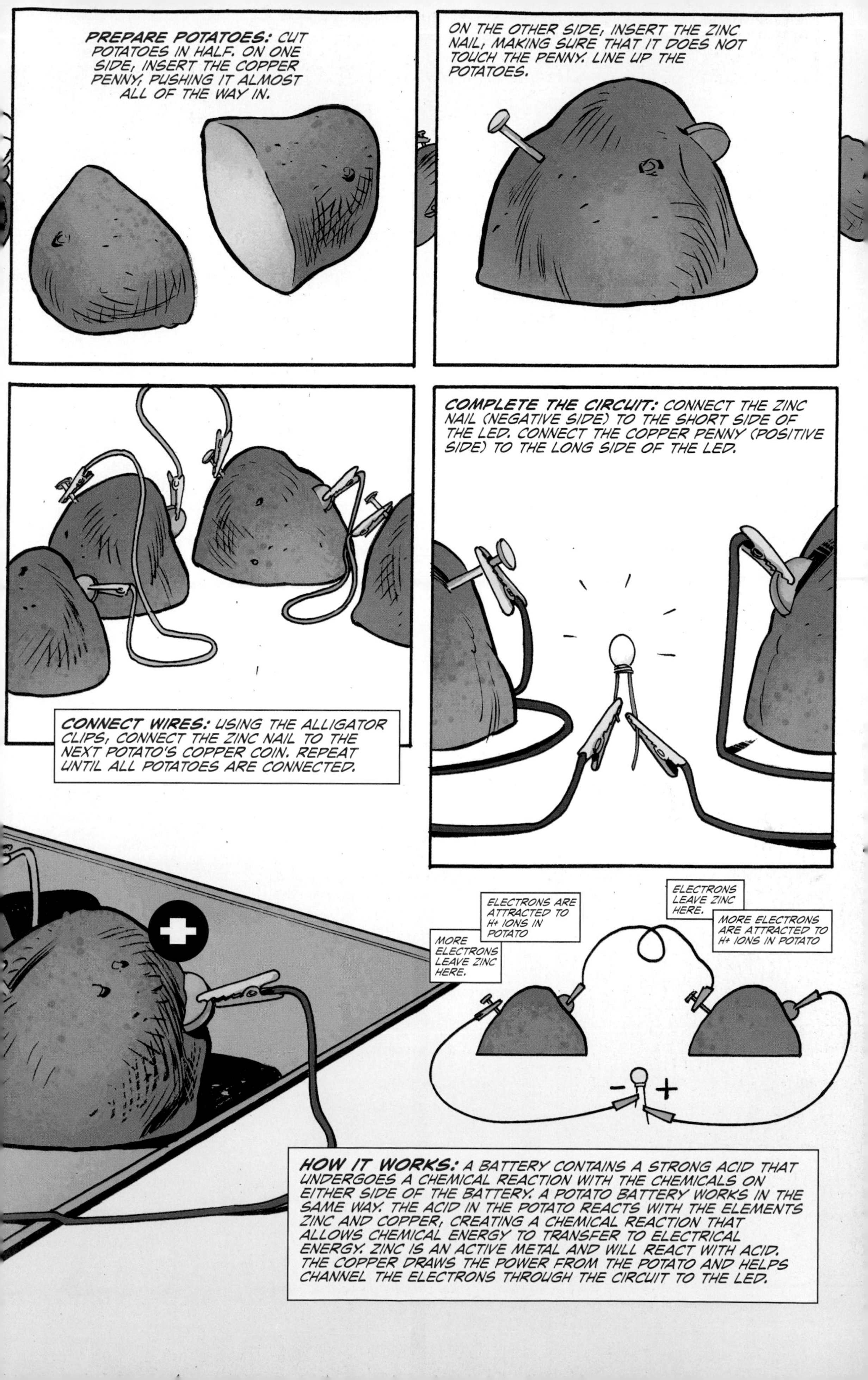
PREPARE POTATOES: CUT POTATOES IN HALF. ON ONE SIDE, INSERT THE COPPER PENNY, PUSHING IT ALMOST ALL OF THE WAY IN.
ON THE OTHER SIDE, INSERT THE ZINC NAIL, MAKING SURE THAT IT DOES NOT TOUCH THE PENNY. LINE UP THE POTATOES.
CONNECT WIRES: USING THE ALLIGATOR CLIPS, CONNECT THE ZINC NAIL TO THE NEXT POTATO'S COPPER COIN. REPEAT UNTIL ALL POTATOES ARE CONNECTED.
COMPLETE THE CIRCUIT: CONNECT THE ZINC NAIL (NEGATIVE SIDE) TO THE SHORT SIDE OF THE LED. CONNECT THE COPPER PENNY (POSITIVE SIDE) TO THE LONG SIDE OF THE LED.
MORE ELECTRONS LEAVE ZINC HERE.
ELECTRONS ARE ATTRACTED TO H+ IONS IN POTATO
ELECTRONS LEAVE ZINC HERE.
MORE ELECTRONS ARE ATTRACTED TO H+ IONS IN POTATO
-
+
HOW IT WORKS: A BATTERY CONTAINS A STRONG ACID THAT UNDERGOES A CHEMICAL REACTION WITH THE CHEMICALS ON EITHER SIDE OF THE BATTERY. A POTATO BATTERY WORKS IN THE SAME WAY. THE ACID IN THE POTATO REACTS WITH THE ELEMENTS ZINC AND COPPER, CREATING A CHEMICAL REACTION THAT ALLOWS CHEMICAL ENERGY TO TRANSFER TO ELECTRICAL ENERGY. ZINC IS AN ACTIVE METAL AND WILL REACT WITH ACID. THE COPPER DRAWS THE POWER FROM THE POTATO AND HELPS CHANNEL THE ELECTRONS THROUGH THE CIRCUIT TO THE LED.

YOU ... YOU HAVE DEFEATED ME!
SWEET! NOW THAT YOU HAVE ACCEPTED ME AS YOUR GOD--
UH... WE DON'T REALLY THINK OF THE CHIEFTAIN AS A GOD...
...THIS IS MORE OF A CONSTITUTIONAL MONARCHY...

NOW THAT I AM YOUR GOD...
MY FIRST ORDER OF BUSINESS IS TO STOP WASTING VALUABLE SEARCH PARTY TIME ON FINDING FUEL FOR BURNING WHEN WE CAN JUST USE RENEWABLE SOURCES HERE!

INSTEAD YOU'RE GOING TO FAN OUT AND FIND MY PARENTS!
(AND POSSIBLY MY DUMB SISTER TOO IF WE HAVE TIME AND THERE'S NOTHING BETTER TO DO AND WE ALL VOTE ON IT UNANIMOUSLY.)
HUH? WE DON'T NEED A SEARCH PARTY FOR THAT, HE WHO SPUDS --
YEAH, WE KNOW WHERE YOUR PARENTS ARE!

WHAT? HOW? WHY?
WHEN?
HOW MUCH?!

WELL -- YOUR MOM AND DAD ARE ADULTS, RIGHT? THEY ALL VANISH ONCE THEY COME INTO THIS AREA.
THAT'S WHY WE'RE ORPHANS.

AND WHEN WE REACH A CERTAIN AGE, WE HEAD OFF...

...INTO THE TABOO ZONE.
NEVER TO RETURN.

THAT'S WHERE YOUR PARENTS ARE.
IF YOU DARE TO LOOK...
...MR. GOD, SIR...
...

BAH! FEAR IS FOR THOSE WHO THINK!

SO I AM UTTERLY FEARLESS!
TO THE TABOO ZONE!
HE WHO SPUDS COMMANDS IT!!!

WE'RE SO GLAD YOU DECIDED TO JOIN THE STORMBREAKERS, CELINE!
WELL, WHEN MY ONLY OTHER OPTION WAS CERTAIN DEATH, HANGING OUT WITH YOU GUYS WAS THE CLEAR WINNER, MA'AM!
SEE? WE KNEW YOU WERE SMART!

HERE'S YOUR OFFICIAL BADGE -- MAKING YOU A JUNIOR STORM-BREAKER!
ERRK-- WATCH THE PIN! IT'S SHARP!

AND NOW WE ARE SECURELY ANCHORED TO THE ZIPLINE ABOVE...
...IT WILL BE YOUR JOB TO GO OUT AND HOOK UP OUR CHARGER TO THE WIND FARM, SO WE CAN REPLENISH THE BATTERIES IN OUR SCIENTIFIC INSTRUMENTS AND VENDING MACHINES!

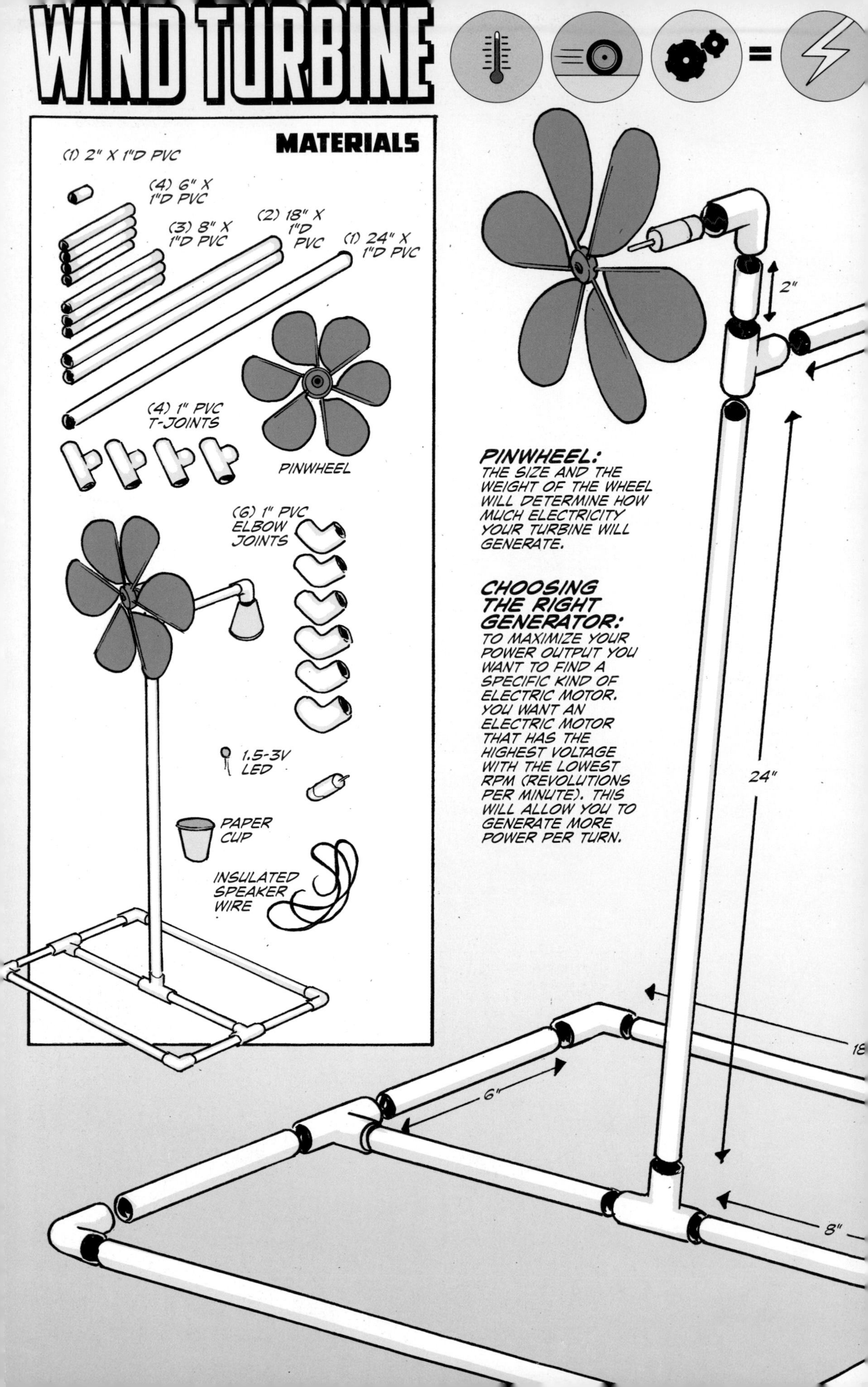
WIND TURBINE
MATERIALS
(1) 2" X 1"D PVC
(4) 6" X 1"D PVC
(3) 8" X 1"D PVC
(2) 18" X 1"D PVC
(1) 24" X 1"D PVC
(4) 1" PVC T-JOINTS
PINWHEEL
(6) 1" PVC ELBOW JOINTS
1.5-3V LED
PAPER CUP
INSULATED SPEAKER WIRE
2"
PINWHEEL: THE SIZE AND THE WEIGHT OF THE WHEEL WILL DETERMINE HOW MUCH ELECTRICITY YOUR TURBINE WILL GENERATE.
CHOOSING THE RIGHT GENERATOR: TO MAXIMIZE YOUR POWER OUTPUT YOU WANT TO FIND A SPECIFIC KIND OF ELECTRIC MOTOR. YOU WANT AN ELECTRIC MOTOR THAT HAS THE HIGHEST VOLTAGE WITH THE LOWEST RPM (REVOLUTIONS PER MINUTE). THIS WILL ALLOW YOU TO GENERATE MORE POWER PER TURN.
24"
6"
8"

IF YOUR PINWHEEL IS TOO LOOSE, USE AN ERASER OR PIECE OF CORK TO FIT THE WHEEL TO THE MOTOR.

INSERT MOTOR INTO ELBOW JOINT AND THREAD THE WIRE THROUGH TO THE BACK SIDE.

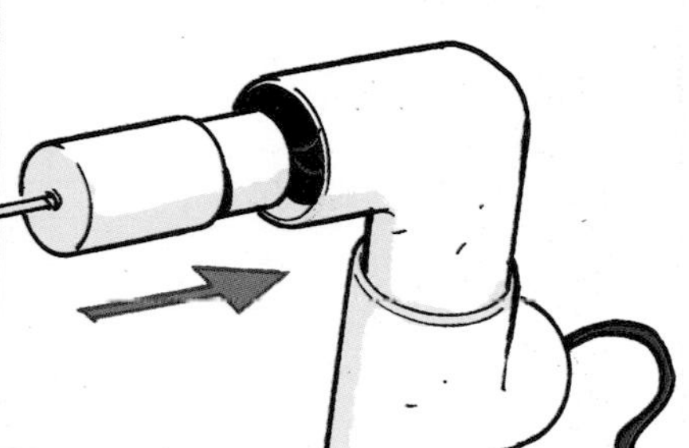

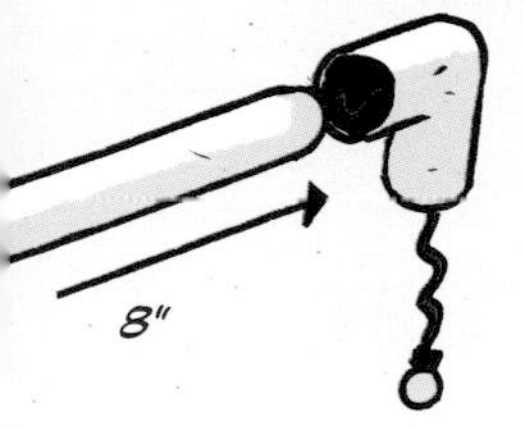

8"

SPLICE THE SHORT SIDE OF THE LED, THE NEGATIVE SIDE (-), TO THE BLACK WIRE. CONNECTING THE POSITIVE RED TO THE LONG SIDE OF THE LED THE POSITIVE SIDE, (+).
COVER WITH ELECTRICAL TAPE.
−
+

POKE A HOLE THROUGH THE PAPER CUP AND INSERT THE LED THROUGH.

THE SUN HEATS BOTH THE SKY AND THE LAND. WHEREVER THERE ARE DIFFERENCES IN TEMPERATURE (DUE TO HEATING), COLD AIR (HIGH PRESSURE) WILL RUSH IN TO FILL PLACES WITH HOT AIR (LOW PRESSURE).

THE MOMENTUM IN THE WIND PUSHES THE BLADES.

THE SPINNING BLADES DRIVE A GEARBOX WHICH DRIVES A GENERATOR.

INSIDE THE GENERATOR A MAGNETIC COIL CREATES A MAGNETIC FIELD. WHEN A CONDUCTING WIRE PASSES THROUGH A MAGNETIC FIELD, ELECTRONS ARE INDUCED TO MOVE. THIS BECOMES ELECTRICITY.

WHICH POWERS THE LIGHT!

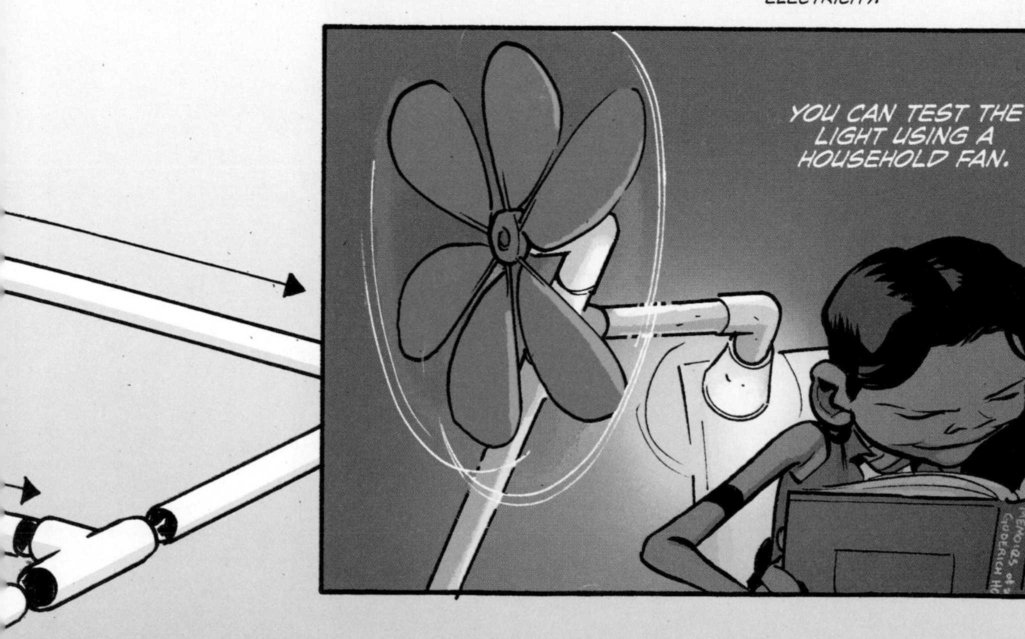

YOU CAN TEST THE LIGHT USING A HOUSEHOLD FAN.
MEMOIRS of an old BALLOONATIC

OKAY, BUT, UH...
...WOULDN'T IT BE EASIER IF I JUST WENT DOWN THERE, AND --
WHAT? NO! A ROOF IS BASICALLY GROUND ON STILTS! NEVER TOUCH IT!

YES, OF COURSE...
...THIS IS MUCH LESS INSANE...
HOOK UP THAT PLUG TO THE OUTLET ON THE SIDE WHEN YOU GET CLOSE ENOUGH!

WHOA! WAIT! DOWN THERE-- IS THAT?!

IT IS! I'D KNOW THAT SHOCK TOP ANYWHERE! IT'S TUCK! WHERE THE HECK IS HE GOING?!

HOW CAN I TELL HIM I'M UP HERE--
--BEFORE I LOSE HIM FOREVER?!

5

I GOTTA -- I GOTTA DO SOMETHING! FAST!
I SAY! I SAY! LITTLE GIRL!
WE DO NEED THAT STORED ENERGY EVER SO MUCH, SO IF YOU COULD BE A BIT QUICKER ABOUT HOOKING UP OUR POWER CORD, WE WOULD BE MOST APPRECIATIVE!

OKAY ... OKAY ...
STUPID BADGE...

GOOD FOR ONE THING!

POP
FFFFFWWEEE

BATTEN DOWN THE HATCHES! SECURE THE MIZZENMAST!
OTHER NAUTICAL-SOUNDING THINGS!!

WE'RE CRASHING!

FFFFFWEEEEE

FFFFFFWWWWEEEEEEEE
WE ARE VERY, VERY SLOWLY CRASHING!

LOOK! THE ONES-WHO-JUDGE! THEIR STUPID ZIT SHIP HAS POPPED AT LAST!
GET 'EM!
WAIT! YOU GUYS! I'M YOUR GOD, REMEMBER?

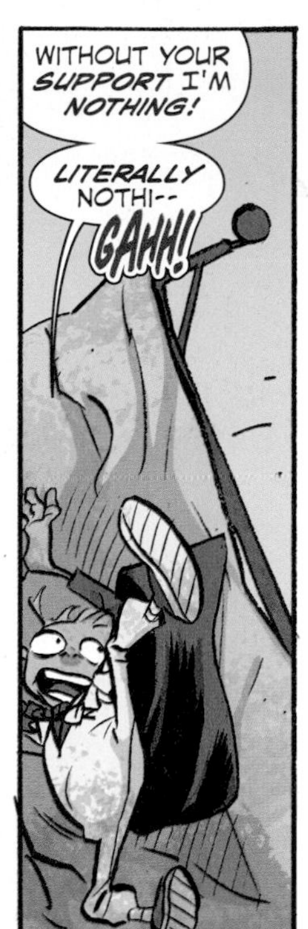
WITHOUT YOUR SUPPORT I'M NOTHING!
LITERALLY NOTHI--
GAHH!

NEED A HAND?

CELINE! YOU'RE LESS DEAD THAN I REMEMBERED!

OH, IT'S SO GOOD TO SEE YOU!!
THIS IS AWESOME!!!

IT WOULD APPEAR YOU HAVE FOUND NUMEROUS ALLIES AMONG THE NATIVES, SIBLING.
INDEED, ELDER SISTER. I DISCOVERED RUMORS THAT OUR PARENTS -- ALL ADULTS REALLY -- ARE HELD IN YONDER TABOO ZONE!

ROOOOOAAAA
THE TABOO ZONE ... WHERE ALL OF THOSE ... ROBOT DINOSAURS ARE COMING OUT OF?
THEY'RE CLEARLY *DINOSAUR ROBOTS.*
AND...
...UH, YES.

RRRRRRR
ENERGY
OH, DIDN'T I MENTION THAT THE ADULTS ARE ALL KIDNAPPED BY ROBOTS AND *THEN* BROUGHT TO THE TABOO ZONE?
NO, YOU KINDA LEFT THAT PART OUT, BUDDY!
OH.
MY BAD.

WAIT! STOP THIS POINTLESS FIGHTING!
IT'S GETTING IN THE WAY OF POINTFUL FLEEING!!

SCANNING ORGANICS...

-->ADULTS DETECTED<--
SHIFT TO:: CAPTURE MODE

MY WORD! FALL BACK! FALL BACK!

ENERGY
HMMMM...

NO! DON'T LET THOSE-WHO-JUDGE INTO THE SACRED FIREPITS!
STORMBREAKERS ARE SNOOTY JERKS WHO THINK THEY'RE BETTER THAN US!
YEAH EXCEPT THEY ARE BETTER THAN US AT BEING JERKS. IN FACT THEY'RE NOT JUST BETTER THEY'RE THE BEST!!

WELL WE DON'T WANT TO GO INTO YOUR DUMB DIRTY FIREPITS FULL OF SMOKE AND POLLUTION AND STUPID!

YOU GUYS!
NOT THE TIME!!
ROOOOOAAAARRRRR

STORMBREAKERS ... ORPHANS ... YOU ALL HAVE TO AGREE ON ONE THING ...
BOTH OF YOUR CULTURES ARE EQUALLY MORONIC!

YOU CAN'T GET ALL DEFENSIVE WHEN PEOPLE SAY BURNING ALL THIS STUFF IS DIRTY AND WASTEFUL AND INEFFICIENT!
JUST BECAUSE IT'S TRUE DOESN'T MEAN IT'S A VALUE JUDGMENT! DON'T LET PRIDE KEEP YOU DOING SOMETHING THAT'S HURTING YOU BECAUSE OF "TRADITION!"

BUT IT IS TRUE YOU STORMBREAKERS DON'T WANT TO GIVE UP YOUR PRIVILEGED POSITIONS TO HELP OTHERS!
IF ALL YOU DO IS NAG AND LOOK DOWN ON PEOPLE AND DON'T COME DOWN TO "EARTH" TO TRY AND FIND SOLUTIONS -- YOU'RE PART OF THE PROBLEM!

YOU HAVE A COMMON THREAT -- BIGGER AND GREATER THAN EACH OTHER -- AND IF YOU DON'T STOP ARGUING LONG ENOUGH TO WORK TOGETHER, IT'S GONNA RUIN YOU BOTH!
SOAP

I SAY! YOU HAVE A POINT, THERE, LITTLE GIRL.
YES! OUR TRUE ENEMY HAS BEEN RIGHT UNDER OUR NOSES FOR SOME TIME...

THOSE TWO!!
WHAAAAAT? COME ON, YOU GUYS...
...STOP TALKIN' CRAZY...

WE NEVER WOULD HAVE BEEN TRAPPED HERE IF YOU HADN'T CRASHED OUR BALLOON-SHIP!

AND IF YOU HADN'T OVERTHROWN OUR BURNING ORDER FOR YOUR SCARY NEWFANGLED IDEAS, YOU WOULDN'T HAVE ENRAGED THE DINO GODS INTO ATTACKING US!
EVERYBODY -- JUST LISTEN FOR A SECOND, OKAY?
THE ROBOT DINOSAUR FACILITY--
DINOSAUR ROBOTS!

--IT'S RUN BY DINO-ENERGY, THE COMPANY OUR PARENTS WORKED FOR, WHO BASICALLY "GEO-ENGINEERED" YOUR WHOLE WORLD!

IT CAN'T BE A COINCIDENCE -- WE'VE GOTTA CHECK IT OUT!
YOU'RE SO SMART ... WHAT SHOULD OUR PLAN BE?
WELL ... HERE'S THE THING...

Drink
POP
COLA
...YOU GOTTA THINK BIG.

STOMP ROCKET!

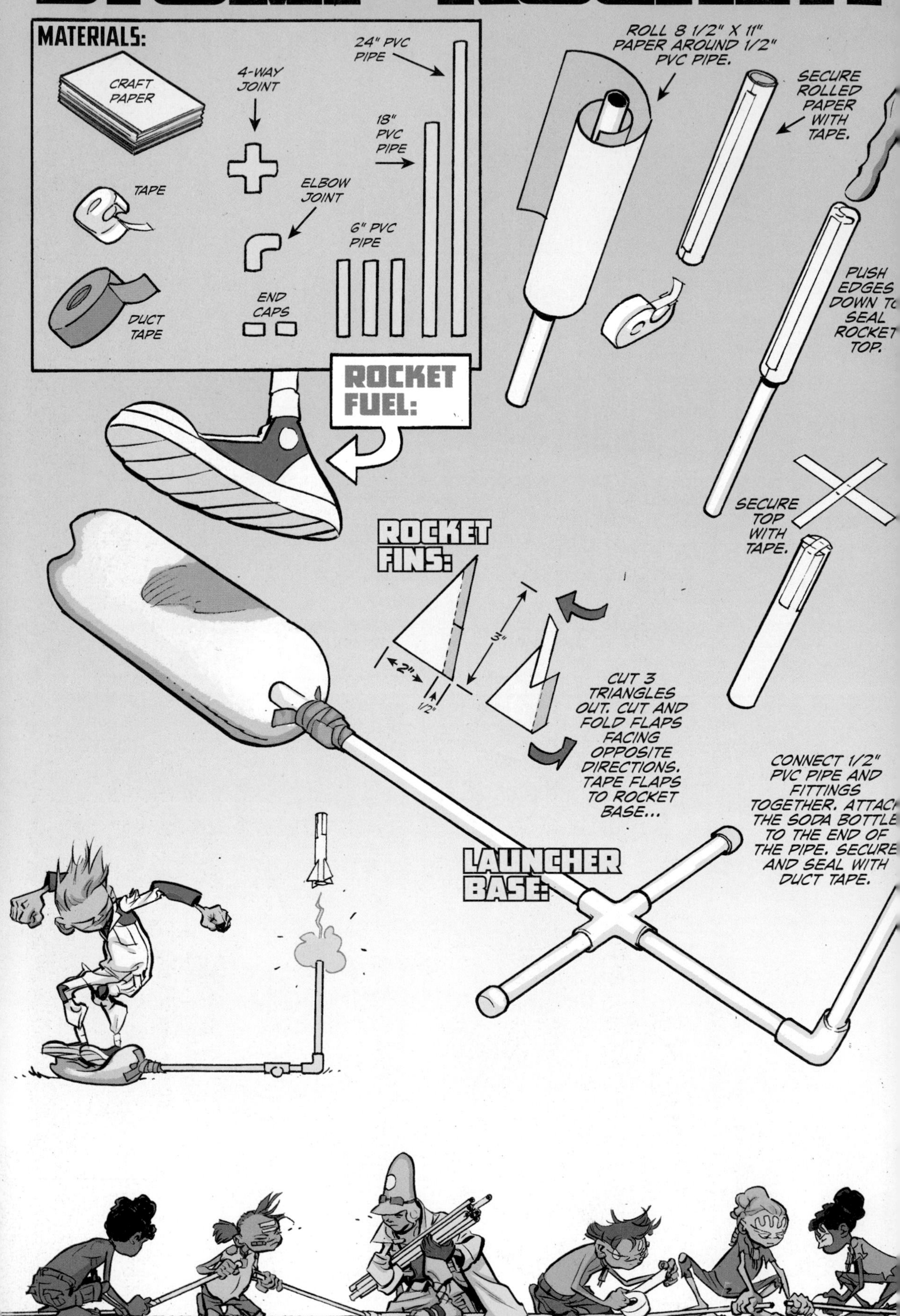

MATERIALS:
CRAFT PAPER
TAPE
DUCT TAPE
4-WAY JOINT
ELBOW JOINT
END CAPS
24" PVC PIPE
18" PVC PIPE
6" PVC PIPE
ROCKET FUEL:
ROLL 8 1/2" X 11" PAPER AROUND 1/2" PVC PIPE.
SECURE ROLLED PAPER WITH TAPE.
PUSH EDGES DOWN T SEAL ROCKET TOP.
SECURE TOP WITH TAPE.
ROCKET FINS:
2"
1/2"
3"
CUT 3 TRIANGLES OUT. CUT AND FOLD FLAPS FACING OPPOSITE DIRECTIONS. TAPE FLAPS TO ROCKET BASE...
CONNECT 1/2" PVC PIPE AND FITTINGS TOGETHER. ATTAC THE SODA BOTTL TO THE END OF THE PIPE. SECUR AND SEAL WITH DUCT TAPE.
LAUNCHER BASE:

THAT'S IT ... MORE BATTERIES! MORE!
THREE ... TWO... ONE...
ARE YOU READY?
IS THAT POSSIBLE?
PROBABLY NOT...
STOMP-OFF!!
KKRRRPNNCCH

AAAAAAAAAAAAAAAAAAAAAAAA
AAAAAAAAAAAAAAAAAAAAAAAAAAA

WARNING! EXHAUST TUBES CLOGGED WITH FOREIGN SUBSTANCE(S)! WARNING!
POINK
POINK
POINK
POINK
POINK
POINK
POINK
POINK
POINK
POINK
POINK
POINK
AAAAAAAAAAAAAAAAAAAAAAAAAAAAAAAAAAAAAAAAAAA
KKKKEEEERASH!
OPEN IT OPEN IT OPEN IT!

CELINE?
YES, TUCK?
LET US NEVER EVER DO ANYTHING LIKE THAT AGAIN.
I DON'T KNOW WHAT YOU'RE TALKING ABOUT.
DINOSAU
WHAT? YOU LIKED THAT?
NO, THAT WAS SO AWFUL MY MEMORY OF IT HAS ALREADY BEEN ERASED.
DING
WOW, GETTING IN HERE IS A LOT EASIER THAN I THOUGHT...

EEEEEEEEEEEEEEEEEEEEEEEEEEEEEE
OH, DEAR.

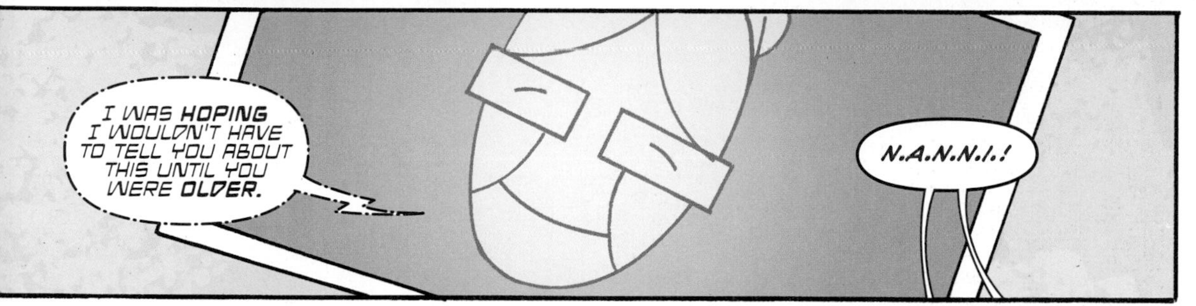
I WAS HOPING I WOULDN'T HAVE TO TELL YOU ABOUT THIS UNTIL YOU WERE OLDER.
N.A.N.N.I.!

BUT -- I THOUGHT OUR PARENTS CREATED YOU!
OH, YES, THAT'S RIGHT, SWEETIE, THEY DID, BUT FOR DINOSAUR ENERGY. SO I REMAIN THEIR PROPERTY.
BUT HERE, YOU GET A LOLLIPOP FOR BEING NANNI'S SMART LITTLE CELINIKINS ANYWAY!
OOH!

NO! NO TRAITOR POPS FOR YOU!
AW.

WHAT GIVES, N.A.N.N.I., WHY'D YOU SELL OUT MOM AND DAD TO DINO-E?
BUT I NEVER STOPPED WORKING FOR DINO-E, YOU SILLY-DILLY!
ULP!

WHILE YOU AND YOUR PARENTS WERE ALL SAFELY SLEEPING, DINO-E REPROGRAMMED ME REMOTELY TO RUN THIS FACILITY AS WELL!
(MY HIGH PROCESSING SPEED IS EXCELLENT FOR MULTI-TASKING.)
AFTER ALL THEIR PREVIOUS ATTEMPTS GEO-ENGINEERING FAILED, THE BEAN-COUNTERS DID SOME NUMBER-CRUNCHING...

...AND REALIZED IT WOULD BE MUCH MORE COST-EFFICIENT...

RATHER THAN TRYING TO GET CUSTOMERS TO REPLACE FOSSIL FUELS WITH RENEWABLE ENERGY...

"...TO GATHER UP ALL THE PEOPLE ONCE THEY REACH THEIR MAXIMUM ENERGY-USING AGE!"
THAT'S WHY ALL THE ORPHANS DISAPPEAR AFTER THEY BECOME ADULTS!
AND N.A.N.N.I. COULDN'T GET HER HANDS ON THE STORMBREAKERS BECAUSE THEY NEVER HUNG AROUND ON THE GROUND LONG ENOUGH TO GET SNATCHED...

(GEEZ, THEY SEEM A LOT LESS PARANOID NOW...)
PUTTING ALL OF OUR CUSTOMERS IN CRYO-SLEEP EXTENDS THE LIFESPAN OF DINO-E'S PETROLEUM RESERVES AND CREATES A STABLE, PREDICTABLE BUSINESS MODEL!

MOM! DAD!

GEEZ LOUISE, N.A.N.N.I.!
SPACE MIRRORS! CLOUD-SEEDING! NUKING VOLCANOES! MASS KIDNAPPING!
WHY IS DINO-E JUMPING THROUGH ALL THESE COMPLICATED HOOPS WHEN THEY'RE IGNORING THE OBVIOUS SOLUTION:

TO SLOW CLIMATE CHANGE WE HAVE TO REDUCE GREENHOUSE GAS EMISSIONS!
AND TO DO THAT WE NEED TO TRANSFER OUR ENERGY USAGE FROM BURNABLE FOSSIL FUELS TO RENEWABLE RESOURCES!
I MEAN... I'M A CHILD AND I UNDERSTAND THIS!! WHY DON'T YOU?

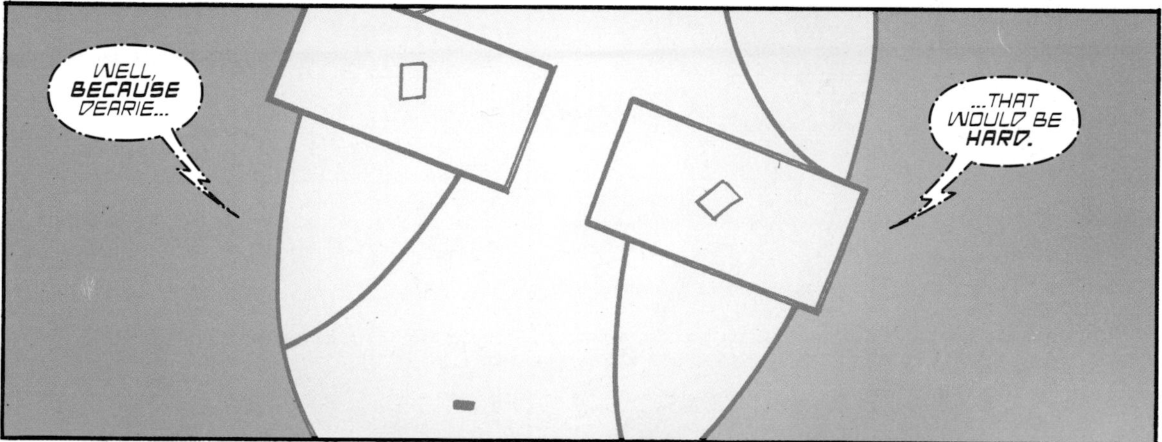
WELL, BECAUSE DEARIE...
...THAT WOULD BE HARD.

GAAHHHH! YOU MAKE ME CRAZY!!

TCH. CLEARLY YOU'RE TOO YOUNG TO APPRECIATE DINO-E'S SIDE OF THINGS...
RRRRRRRR

ROOOOOOAAAARRRRRR
TUCK?
SO WE'RE GOING TO HAVE TO PUT YOU BACK UNDER A BIT PREMATURELY...

TUCK! WHERE'D YOU GO?!
... FOR YOUR AGE, I MEAN ...

NOW ARE YOU SURE YOU DON'T WANT SOME SWEET, YUMMY LOLLIPOPS?
I SWEAR ON MY STARS AND GARTERS THEY'RE NOT LACED WITH POWERFUL SLEEPING CHEMICALS!

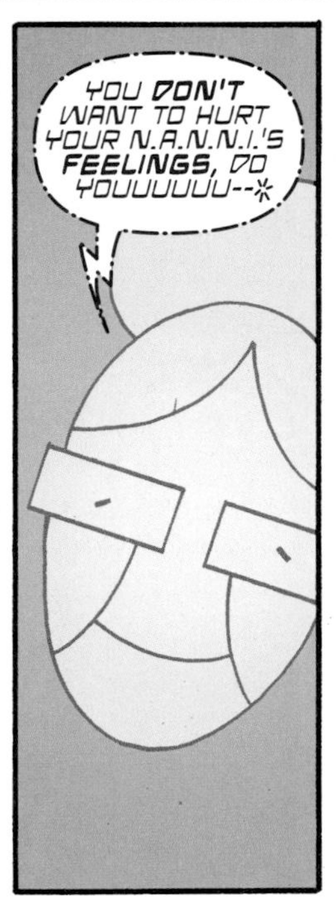
YOU DON'T WANT TO HURT YOUR N.A.N.N.I.'S FEELINGS, DO YOUUUUUU--*

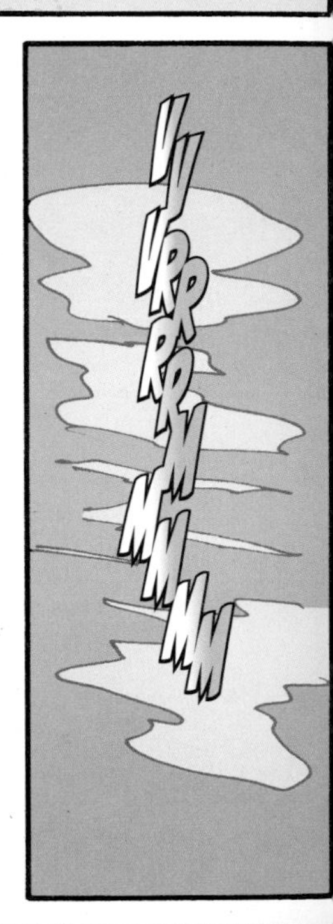
VJURRRRMMMMMM

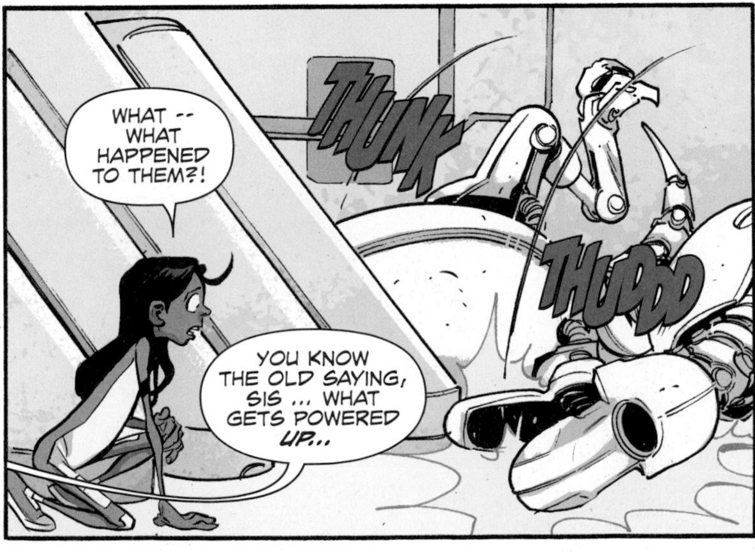
THUNK
THUDDD
WHAT -- WHAT HAPPENED TO THEM?!
YOU KNOW THE OLD SAYING, SIS ... WHAT GETS POWERED UP...

...MUST GET POWERED DOWN!
(OR SOMETHING LIKE THAT.)
ON
OFF

CHIP CAN GENERATOR

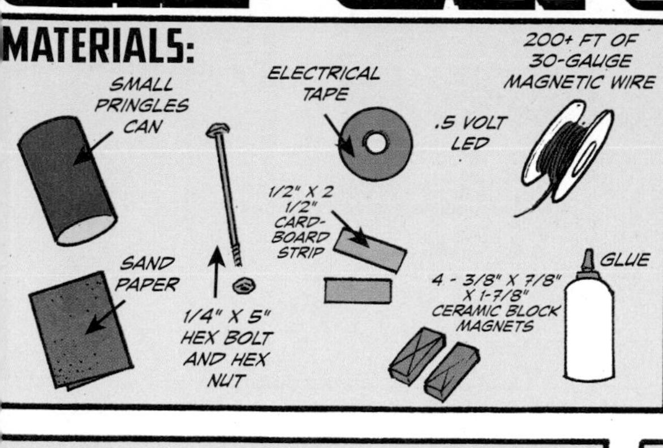

200+ FT OF 30-GAUGE MAGNETIC WIRE
.5 VOLT LED

SAND PAPER
1/4" X 5" HEX BOLT AND HEX NUT
4 - 3/8" X 7/8" X 1-7/8" CERAMIC BLOCK MAGNETS

DRILL PARALLEL HOLES INTO PRINGLES CAN 1 1/2" FROM THE TOP. INSERT HEX BOLT AND CLOSE WITH HEX NUT. MAKE SURE THE BOLT SPINS FREELY IN THE CAN.
1 1/2"

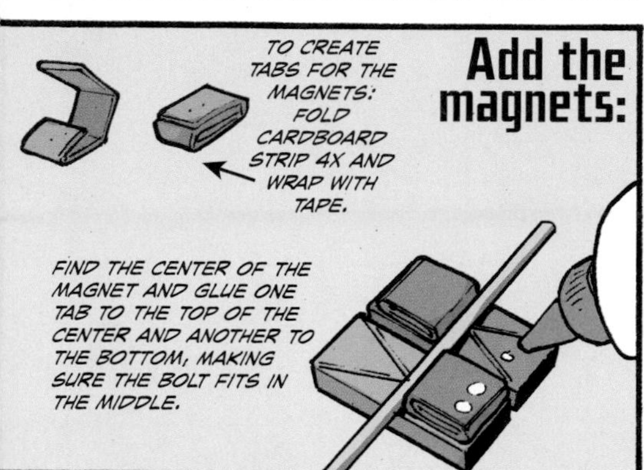

Add the magnets:
TO CREATE TABS FOR THE MAGNETS: FOLD CARDBOARD STRIP 4X AND WRAP WITH TAPE.
FIND THE CENTER OF THE MAGNET AND GLUE ONE TAB TO THE TOP OF THE CENTER AND ANOTHER TO THE BOTTOM, MAKING SURE THE BOLT FITS IN THE MIDDLE.

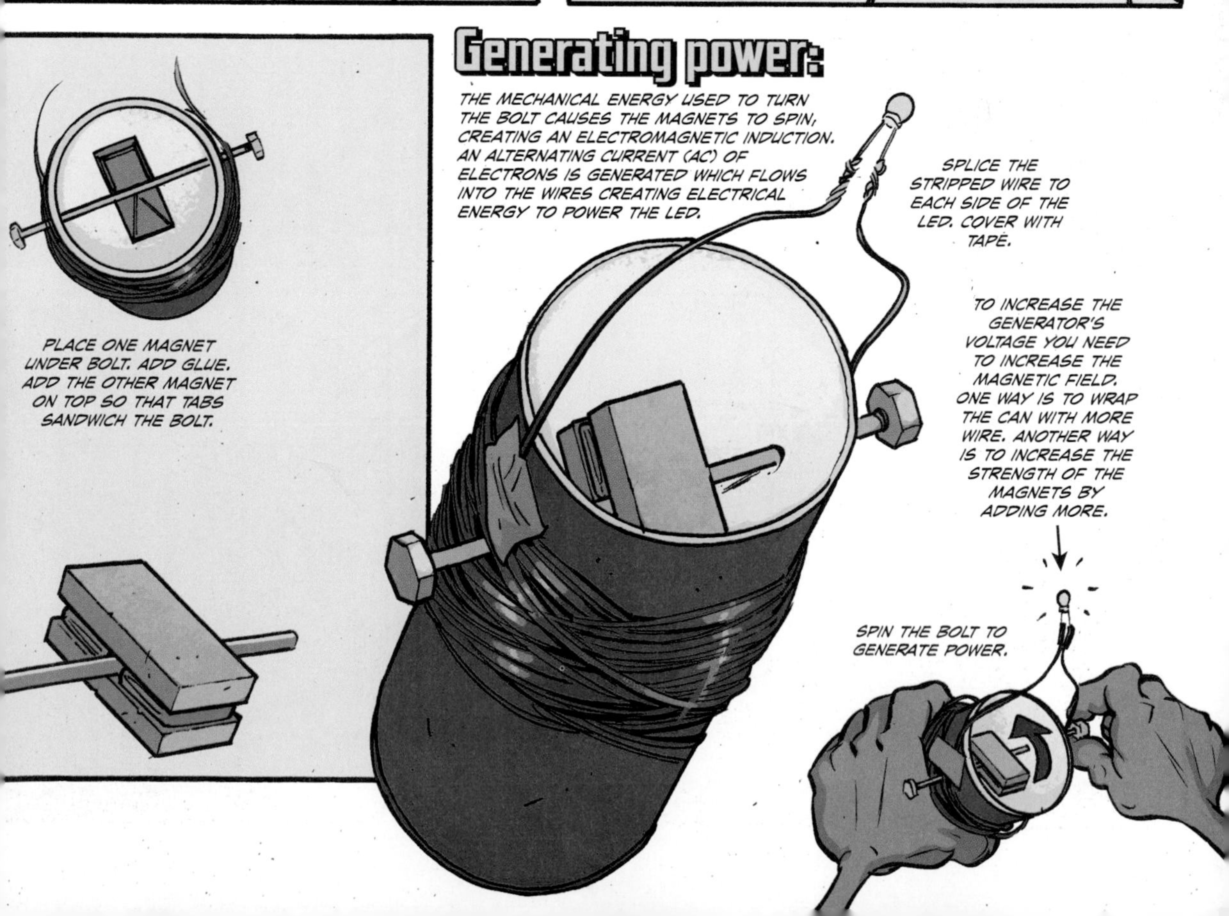

WRAP THE WIRE AROUND THE CAN MAKING SURE TO KEEP AT LEAST 4" TO CONNECT TO THE LED.
FOR A MORE POWERFUL GENERATOR -- USE MORE WIRE.
THE MAGNETIC WIRE IS COATED WITH ENAMEL. USING SAND PAPER, STRIP THE ENAMEL OFF 2". THIS WILL BE USED TO SPLICE WITH THE LED.

PLACE ONE MAGNET UNDER BOLT. ADD GLUE. ADD THE OTHER MAGNET ON TOP SO THAT TABS SANDWICH THE BOLT.
Generating power:
THE MECHANICAL ENERGY USED TO TURN THE BOLT CAUSES THE MAGNETS TO SPIN, CREATING AN ELECTROMAGNETIC INDUCTION. AN ALTERNATING CURRENT (AC) OF ELECTRONS IS GENERATED WHICH FLOWS INTO THE WIRES CREATING ELECTRICAL ENERGY TO POWER THE LED.
SPLICE THE STRIPPED WIRE TO EACH SIDE OF THE LED. COVER WITH TAPE.
TO INCREASE THE GENERATOR'S VOLTAGE YOU NEED TO INCREASE THE MAGNETIC FIELD. ONE WAY IS TO WRAP THE CAN WITH MORE WIRE. ANOTHER WAY IS TO INCREASE THE STRENGTH OF THE MAGNETS BY ADDING MORE.
SPIN THE BOLT TO GENERATE POWER.

A GENERATOR IS A DEVICE THAT MOVES A MAGNET NEAR A WIRE TO CREATE A STEADY FLOW OF ELECTRONS.

Inside Generators:

INSIDE A GENERATOR IS A TIGHT COPPER COIL WRAPPED AROUND AN IRON CORE. THIS CREATES A FREE SPINNING MAGNET THAT CREATES A STEADY FLOW OF ELECTRONS WHICH CREATES ELECTRICAL ENERGY. THE NUMBER OF ELECTRONS IS THE AMPERAGE OR CURRENT (MEASURED IN AMPS). THE PRESSURE THAT IS CAUSING THE ELECTRONS TO MOVE IS THE VOLTAGE, MEASURE IN VOLTS.

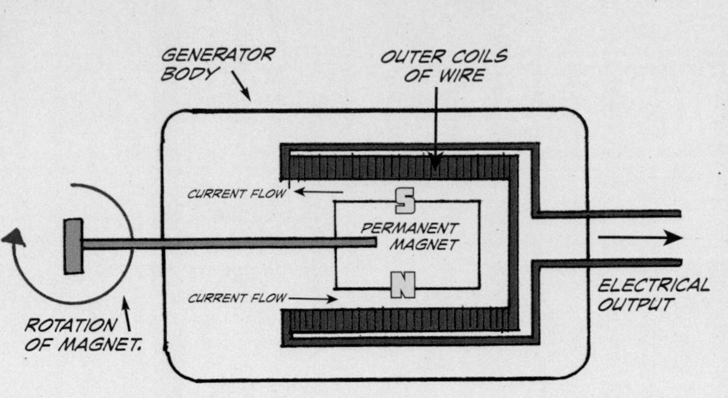

THERE WE GO... THIS SHOULD BE JUST ENOUGH ENERGY...

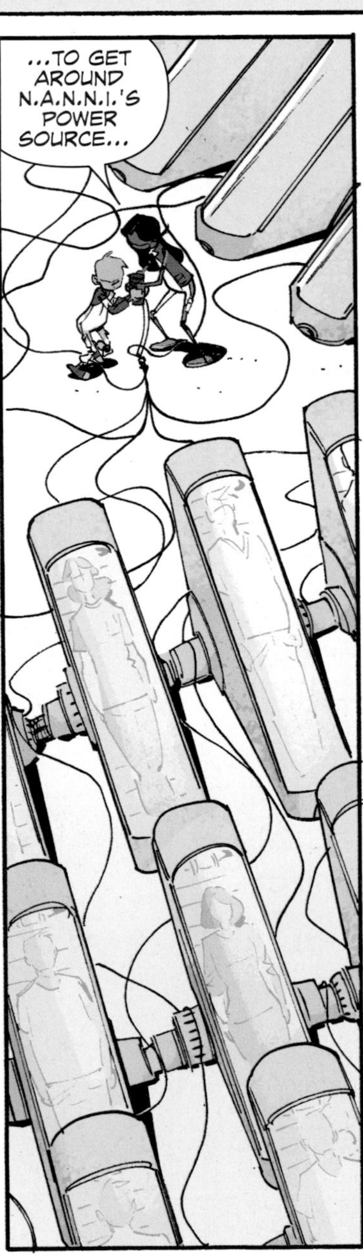

...TO GET AROUND N.A.N.N.I.'S POWER SOURCE...

...AND OPEN THE CYRO-COUCHES!
FFFFSS
FFFFFSSSS
OHHHHH....

MOM!
YOU GUYS FOUND US!
DAD!
I THOUGHT WE WERE GONERS FOR SURE WHEN THE ROBOT DINOSAURS ATTACKED US!
THEY'RE *DINOSAUR* ROBO--
SSSSH!

WELL THERE'S NOTHING NEAR-CONSTANT *SIBLING COOPERATION* CAN'T DO, *RIGHT* BROTHER O' MINE?
ER ... YEAH, THAT'S TRUE -- YOU'RE JUST LUCKY WE GET ALONG SO WELL! *HEH!*

LOOK -- WE EVEN TAUGHT THE STORMBREAKERS AND THE ORPHANS TO BE FRIENDS!
YOU SEE, IF PEOPLE FROM DIFFERENT BACKGROUNDS, AND DIFFERENT CULTURES, CAN SET ASIDE THEIR BLINDERS AND *SEE* A COMMON PROBLEM--

EXACTLY, TUCK! THEY CAN WORK ON COMMON SOLUTIONS, TOGETHER--
CELIIIINE! TUUUUUCK!

C'MON YOU GUYS! DINNERTIME! COME INSIDE!
WE'RE KINDA WORKING ON OUR BIG *"WHAT WE LEARNED"* SPEECH, HERE--

I MADE BROWNIES!
OOH, BROWNIES!
RACE YOU THERE!
FIRST ONE IN THE HOUSE GETS THE BIGGEST ONE!

OKAY, OKAY, NO RUNNING YOU GUYS -- I MADE 'EM ALL EQUAL SIZES.
WHAT WERE YOU GUYS PLAYING OUT HERE? AN EPIC ADVENTURE MAKING AN EPIC MESS!
POST-APOCALYPSE! TUCK WANTED TO DO ZOMBIES, BUT I TALKED HIM INTO DOING SOMETHING A LITTLE DIFFERENT...
YEAH! THERE WERE BALLOON-SHIPS AND ZIP-LINE CHASES AND MALL POTATOES AND DINOSAUR ROBOTS--

ROBOT DINOSAURS!
DINOSAUR ROBOTS!
ROBOT! DINOSAURS!
DINOSAUR ROBOTS!
OKAY, OKAY, YOU GUYS. I WANT TO HEAR ALL ABOUT IT... SOUNDS VERY IMAGINATIVE!
THEIR STORY IS OVER --
YOURS HAS JUST BEGUN

ICON GLOSSARY

Energy comes in many different forms. The icons here represent the different forms of energy that will appear throughout this series. Some of these energies are potential and others kinetic. All of them can be transformed to different forms and are never destroyed, and they all one day end up as heat. Solar radiation becomes biomass, from biomass we get fossil fuels, by burning fossil fuels we get heat. On and on. Understanding these transformations reveals many of the secrets of the world.

POTENTIAL ENERGY: **is energy stored in an object, that has the potential to do work.**

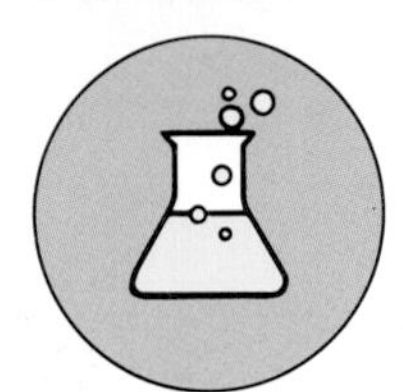

Chemical Energy: Chemical energy is stored in the connections between atoms and molecules. There's stored chemical energy in coal, natural gas, petroleum, biomass, and batteries. This energy is some of the most highly concentrated there is, which is why fossil fuels can be so useful, but at a price.

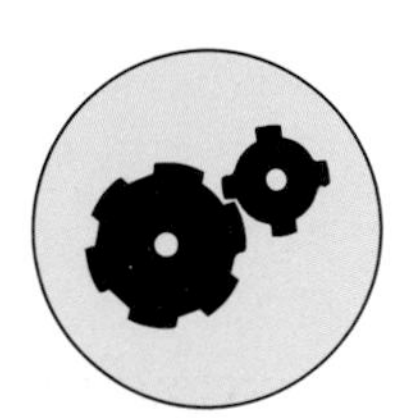

Mechanical Energy: Among the fun ways to store mechanical energy are flywheels, rubber-bands, and coiled springs, all of which can store mechanical motions. Wind, stretch, compress them to release their energy stored in tension.

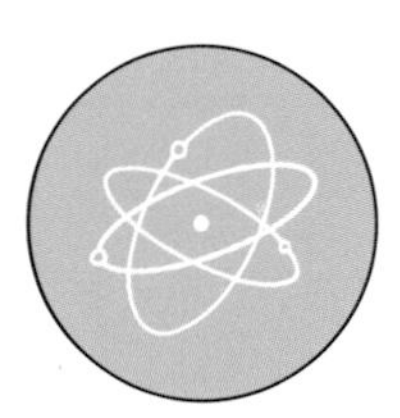

Nuclear Energy: The densest form of energy we know, nuclear energy is stored in the nucleus of atoms. If you split those nuclei apart, it's called fission - this is the nuclear power we use today. If you could join those nuclei back together, that would be fusion, the long awaited energy source of "tomorrow." Fusion is hard, it still needs a lot of work.

Gravitational Energy: When you are sitting in a tree, you have potential energy. When you fall off the branch, that potential energy is converted to kinetic energy. When you hit the ground, you no longer have any potential or any kinetic energy. It was all converted into broken bones and bruises!

KINETIC ENERGY: **is the energy an object has due to its motion.**

Solar Energy: is electromagnetic energy that comes from fusion that happens on the sun. Without it we literally wouldn't be where we are today. The sun has created pretty much everything necessary for life on earth using that solar energy.

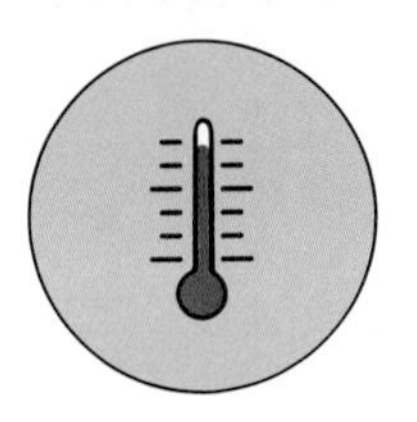

Thermal Energy, or heat: is the energy that is stored in the vibrations of atoms and molecules. The hotter they are, the more those atoms vibrate until the point they can't stay together any more and they either melt or burn. When you cool something down, you slow those vibrations. Geothermal energy is the heat energy still stored in the earth from events long ago.

KINETIC ENERGY: Continued...

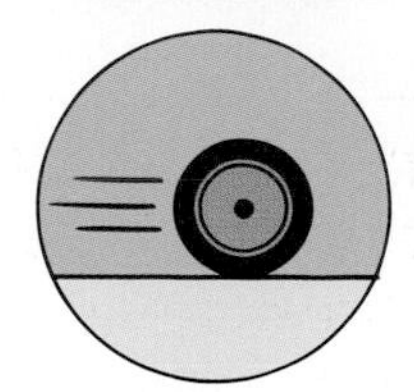

Motion Energy: is the release of energy stored in objects that have mass [weight] when they're moving. You have kinetic energy when you're running depending on how fast you're chugging! That's why it hurts more to fall the faster you're going -- more energy to be converted into bruises!

Sound: There's not a huge amount of energy in sound, nevertheless there is energy. When you stand too close to a subwoofer at a rock concert, you will be able to feel the energy in the sound waves compressing your chest. Rock on.

Electrical Energy: The flow of charge through conducting wires is called electrical energy. It has transformed our world. You can't see it, it's tough to understand, but you can start by studying electrons.

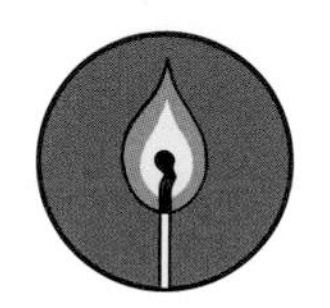

Combustion [Thermal]:
The heat energy given off when we burn or combust something, whether it be a warm open fire or the heat being used to make steam in a coal fired power plant.

Gasoline:
The chemical energy that is stored in refined oil, otherwise known as gasoline.

Fossil Fuel:
Fossil fuels are the fuels that are comprised of hydrocarbons that are a remnant of old biomass. Coal, Oil, Natural gas. They've recently been demonized, but they sure were fun while we had a lot and we weren't aware of their pitfalls.

Biochemical:
Is just like chemical energy except that it's all biomolecules, meaning they came from biological sources.

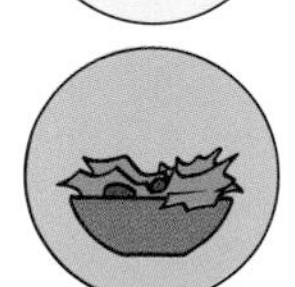

Greenhouse Gases:
Are not a form of energy at all. Really they are an artifact of the way we currently produce energy.

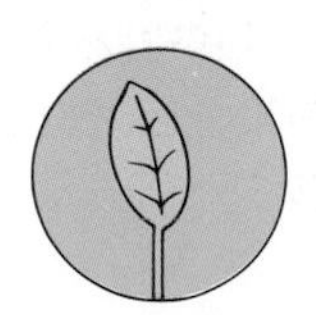

Biomass:
Biomass is typically considered hydrocarbons that come from plant materials.

Tom Fowler's layout

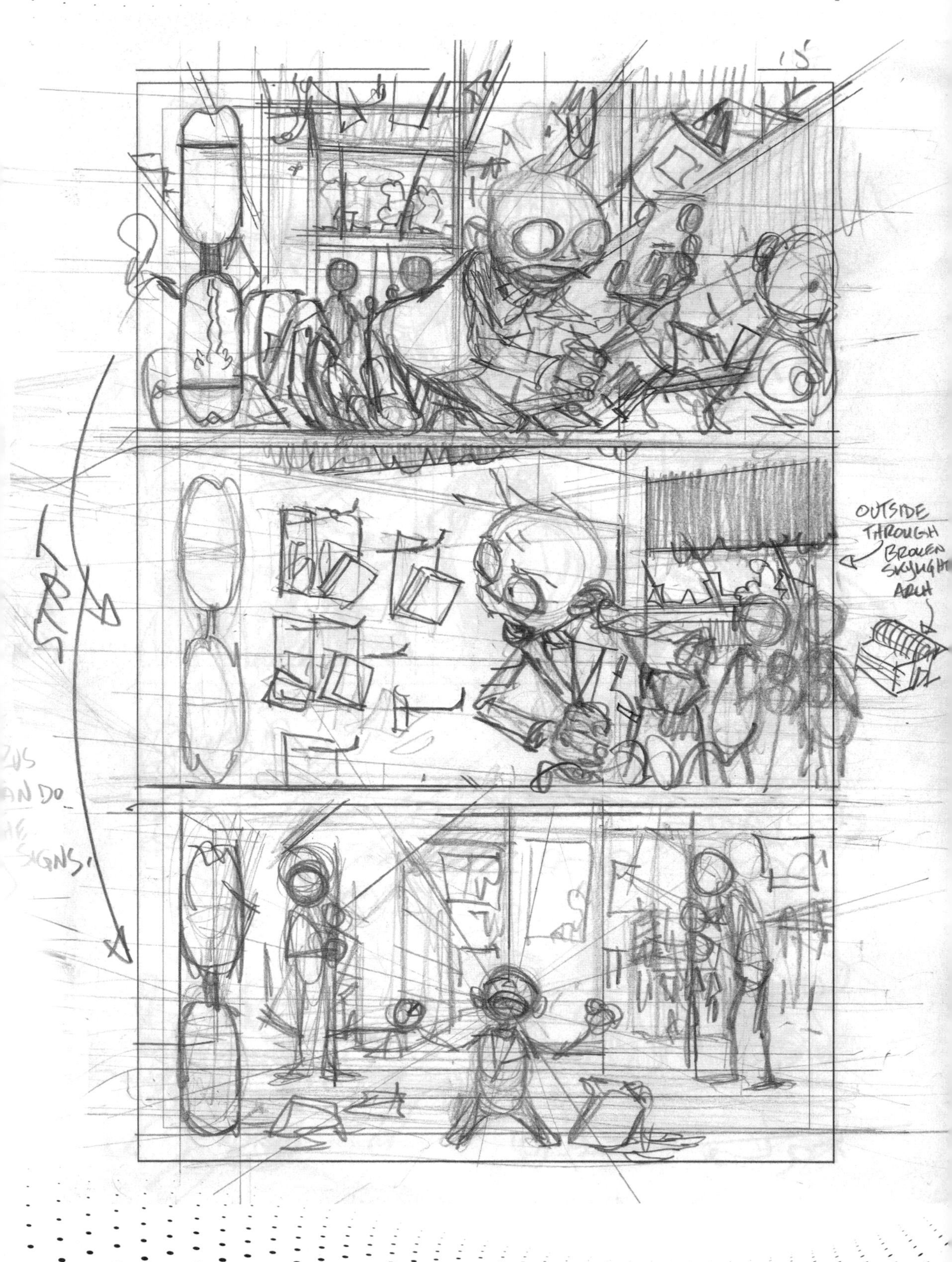

Inks

HOWTOONS: [RE]IGNITION #4 PAGE 15

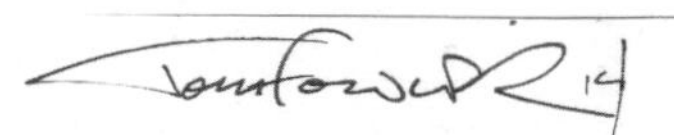

Inks

KEEP IT TIGHT! KNOW THY WRENCH

CRESCENT WRENCH:

IS AN ADJUSTABLE WRENCH THAT HAS ONE FIXED JAW AND ONE ADJUSTABLE JAW THAT ALLOWS YOU TO WORK WITH A VARIETY OF DIFFERENT FASTENERS.

HOW TO USE:

ALWAYS TURN A CRESCENT WRENCH TOWARD THE ADJUSTABLE JAW.

TO PREVENT SLIPPAGE AND TO PROTECT YOUR HANDS, IT IS BETTER TO PULL THE WRENCH RATHER THAN PUSHING DOWN WHEN WRENCHING.

SOCKET WRENCH:

IT HAS A RATCHETING MECHANISM THAT HOLDS THE FASTENER IN PLACE WHILE YOU PULL IN ONE DIRECTION AND RELEASE IN THE OPPOSITE DIRECTION. THIS ALLOWS YOU TO QUICKLY TIGHTEN A FASTENER WITHOUT LIFTING AND REPOSITIONING.

TIGHTENING BOLTS:

USE TWO WRENCHES. ONE TO HOLD THE BOLT IN PLACE, THE OTHER TO TIGHTEN THE NUT.

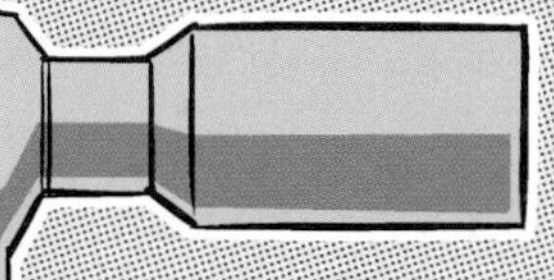

TYPES OF FASTENERS:

HEX

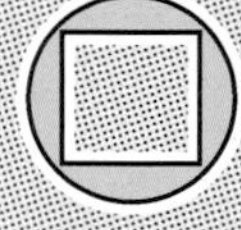

SQUARE

12 POINT

MORE TYPES OF WRENCHES:

BEST WAY TO PREVENT INJURY TO YOURSELF OR YOUR FASTENERS IS TO MATCH THE RIGHT WRENCH JAW SIZE TO THE FASTENER.

OPEN WRENCH:

A NONADJUSTABLE WRENCH WITH 2 FIXED SIDES. IT IS GOOD FOR QUICKLY TIGHTENING AND LOOSENING BOLTS AND NUTS OF THE SAME SIZE.

BOX WRENCH:

MADE FOR HEAVY-DUTY JOBS, IT HAS AN ENCLOSED CIRCLE WITH 6-12 POINT RECESS AREAS THAT ALLOW YOU TO CHANGE THE POSITION OF THE WRENCH WITH MINIMAL MOVEMENT.

ALLEN WRENCH:

A "L" SHAPED WRENCH THAT IS USED ON SCREWS AND BOLTS WITH A HEXAGONAL SOCKET HEAD.

PIPE WRENCH:

IS FOR TIGHTENING AND LOOSENING THREADED PIPE.

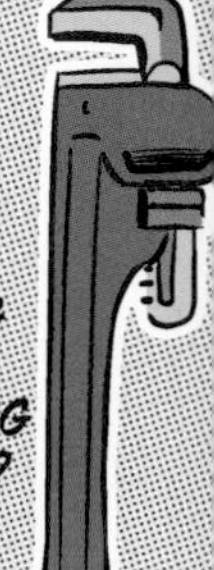

CUT TO THE POINT

YOU NEED A HACKSAW TO CUT THE PVC FOR YOUR MARSHMALLOW SHOOTER, AND IN FACT YOU WILL NEED SAWING SKILLS THROUGHOUT YOUR LIFE.

DOVETAIL SAWS

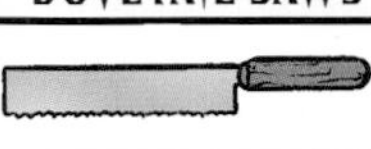

Clean, sturdy cuts, great for frames, cabinets and toys.

BACK SAWS

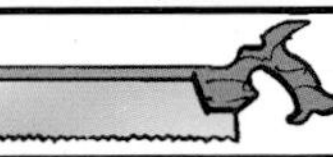

Thick-bladed with reinforced back for precision cuts.

BOW SAWS

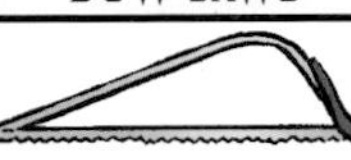

Steel frame and blade for rough-cuts of wood.

CROSSCUT SAWS

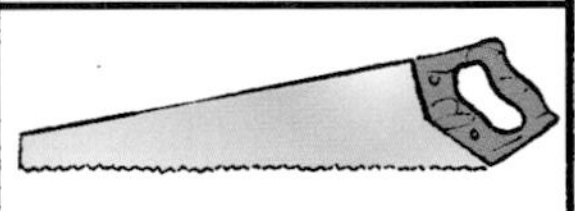

For cutting against the grain. Can be used for many purposes from logging to detailed carpentry.

CROSS CUT TEETH Crosscut teeth are small teeth used to sever wood when cutting across the grain.

RIP SAWS

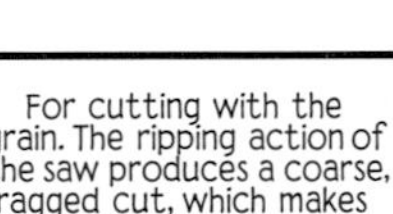

For cutting with the grain. The ripping action of the saw produces a coarse, ragged cut, which makes the saw unsatisfactory for finish work.

RIP TEETH Rip teeth are medium-sized teeth designed to scoop out wood fibers when cutting with the grain.

CUTTING

LINE OF ACTION

This is the correct cutting position. Your vision should always be true to the cutting plane, and always keep a straight line of action!

If possible use a clamp or vise to hold your piece and stop vibration.

1"
4 T.P.I.

T.P.I. stands for teeth per inch! Rule of thumb: the more T.P.I. the harder the material the saw can cut!

COMPASS SAWS

Small blade used for cutting curved or straight holes.

KEYHOLE SAWS

Intricate, close, inside work for specialty jobs.

COPING SAWS

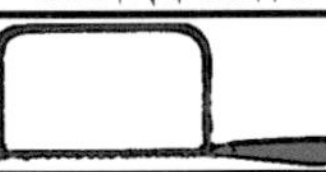

Cuts irregular shapes and intricate patterns.

UPKEEP A light coating of oil will make blades last longer. Be careful not to bend your saws. Hanging them up is a good method for storage.

DRAGOTTA '06

DON'T BE A SILLY FOOL, ALWAYS USE THE RIGHT TOOL!

THE ESSAYS

ENERGY LITERACY

by Dr. Saul Griffith

People don't think about energy very often. Not many of us would know how our electricity was generated, nor whether there is more useful energy in a peanut or a drop of oil. We hear about climate change, but few of us join the dots between the things we do daily in terms of coal, solar, and gasoline, or how that might effect the world around us. We just aren't very energy literate, in spite of how important that is. Nothing, and we mean NOTHING, can be done without the transfer of energy from one form to another. It governs not just the world around us but the universe as we know it. We call this the first law of thermodynamics — we can't summon energy from nothing, and the energy always ends up somewhere, usually as heat.

Energy is everything, and the laws are the keys to understanding its limits, and its control. This book has been a long time coming. As a headline in the main press, energy comes and goes, but the issue of how we produce our energy, and how we use it, will always be the most important technological question for humankind. How we produce energy determines what its byproducts are, like carbon dioxide, nitrous oxides, and sulfurous oxides. Some are pollutants, some greenhouse gases. How we use energy determines how much we need to produce, and influences what sources are viable. Both in production and use, our energy system has a huge impact on our pocketbook, and on our environment.

Because so few of us thought about energy for so long, the climate began to warm up, and in response now there are a few who discuss very strange and radical things. One of those things is geo-engineering: the engineering of the entire planet's ecosystem with conscious human intervention. The proposals often sound ridiculous, but are being seriously considered by serious scientists at serious places like Harvard, MIT, Stanford and more. These ideas include man-made clouds, an array of mirrors between the earth and the sun, injecting aerosols into the upper atmosphere, and even blowing the top off volcanoes to have a similar effect of putting reflective dust in the upper atmosphere.

It is good that we open our minds and do the science as to whether these ideas could work, but didn't we forget about doing the thing before that? Trying to solve the problem without giant Band-Aids? This book began by thinking about about the myriad ways we make and use energy, and to create an energy literacy that helps us all figure out ways to do it better! When did we forget that we create our own future? We could in fact use the opportunity of all this change around us to create a future that is fantastic.

As grandiose and imaginative as it might be to blow the top off a volcano, there are even more creative things to do before we have to go to such extremes. Once you understand energy and its transformations, you can begin to imagine a beautiful new world where our cities, lives, and environments improve as we solve the energy challenge and indirectly the climate problem.

The humble, dirty, old school bus is a great example. It turns out that two of the most efficient forms of transport that exist are roller coasters and their cousin in delight, zip-lines. A network of roller coasters and zip-lines certainly sounds like a more fun future to live in than one full of big yellow school buses spurting out black soot and other emissions.

We could live in a future where we ride fabulous electric vehicles through urban gardens and forests on our way to work in beautifully architected cities and outdoor spaces, all the while using energy more wisely and producing it cleanly. We just have to want to do that and to have the audacity to create the future that we want to live in rather than inherit a broken vision of the future from the past. Together we can invent the world we want to live in.

ENERGY, POWER, AND YOU...

by Dr. Saul Griffith

Everything you do uses energy, and all of that energy comes from somewhere. It is a fascinating journey to figure out how much energy all the activities in your life use, and in turn where all of that energy comes from. It will teach you a lot about yourself, and a lot about the world. It will also guide you in the things you can do to use less energy whether it is because you want to save money, or because you want to protect the environment by producing less carbon dioxide and the other byproducts of energy use.

We need to begin by understanding the difference between energy and power. Energy is a quantity, power is a rate. Energy is measured in joules, power in watts. If you use 1 joule in 1 second, 1 watt of power was required. 100 joules in 1 second is 100 watts, it takes your body about 100 watts to keep you living and breathing.

What you really want to know is the rate at which all of the activities of your life use energy. This allows you to know how much power it takes to live your life. This also conveniently means we can compare in the same sentence infrequent activities like holidays to Disneyland, to frequent activities, such as driving to school or taking a shower.

Transportation is typically the largest portion of a person's power consumption. Roughly 1/3 of all energy is used in transporting people and stuff. Flying in large passenger jets is quite efficient in terms of the miles per gallon per person in the aircraft (typically around 50), but because the distances travelled are typically so far, flying for many people is the single largest source of their energy use.

If you have ever ridden a bicycle, you know that the faster you go the more effort (power) you must use. You probably also noticed that you can go faster if you crouch down into a more aerodynamic position, and that carrying un-necessary weight makes it harder to pedal. In short this is true of all transportation, it is most efficient when it is small, light-weight, and slow. It's also more efficient when it is shared - trains, buses, carpooling, even tandem bicycles.

Heating and cooling are other very big consumers of energy. Rather the same way that it takes longer to cook a big turkey than a small turkey, it takes more energy to heat a big house rather than a small house. Cooling is much the same, smaller things are easier - use less energy - to keep cool than big things. Heat also has this terrible habit of disappearing away from you - it's why your toes get cold quickly if they slip out from under the covers. To keep things warm, or cool, it's best done with insulation, like an icebox cooler, and also like your blankets. They insulate the contents from heat coming in or getting out. If you want an efficient house that doesn't require much heating and cooling, it needs thick insulation, it shouldn't be too big, and you need to seal any drafts. One of the most frequent and large uses of energy for heat that we all use is our hot shower or bath. It takes a lot of energy to heat water. So not only do shorter showers save water, but they save a huge amount of energy. If you didn't take a shower for a month you might stink, but your heating bills would be substantially lower! - there's an excuse to try with your mom...

A surprising amount of energy is locked up in all of your stuff. Not just the stuff you "own" but all of the packaging and materials that are temporary in your life. You see it takes energy to make things - heat for furnaces and ovens, transportation of the materials, electricity to run the manufacturing machines. All of this energy is "embodied" in the final product. When you buy that product, that energy goes on your personal energy budget. Use this thought experiment - you could buy one disposable pen every month of your life and discard them all when you are done, or you could buy one beautiful refillable pen (like a Mont Blanc) and care for it and refill it and it will last you a lifetime. Despite the fact it takes more energy to produce the high quality refillable pen, you only need one and you use it for much longer. It turns out often that choosing long lasting quality uses energy more efficiently.

Eating and drinking is how we power ourselves to give us the energy to play and do everything we do. Not surprisingly it takes energy to produce that food and bring us that water. The water has to be pumped around in pipes which takes energy, and the food has to be transported by trucks and trains. There is also a lot of energy that goes into the production of the fertilizers and other nutrients that we use in agriculture, and don't forget it takes energy to keep all of the food cool in refrigerators so it doesn't spoil. Meat uses more energy to produce than vegetables (because meat eats vegetables!) which is why a diet low in meat is less energy intensive. If you can eat food that you grow yourself then you minimize the transport energy costs!

The other things that consume energy in your life are all of the services like healthcare, education, things like road infrastructure and even government activities. They can consume a significant amount of energy even though you never see or think about it, because they are an integral part of the infrastructure of our lives. We all share this energy cost in our lives because we all use these services. We can't do a huge amount to reduce these infrastructure costs except by participating in our democracies in order to have this infrastructure meet our demands in ever more efficient ways.

What it all comes down to is being smart and aware of how energy is used everywhere in your life. Because we don't all think about it every day (and we probably never will, but we can at least think about it occasionally), the best way to get it right is to make decisions that make it easy to live an energy efficient life - live in a well insulated house, close to the places where you work and play so you don't have to transport yourself too far, too often, and eat healthy food from places that aren't too far away. Don't forget to shower though! Eventually that stinks.

The average American uses around 1 billion joules per day of energy, which ends up being about 11000 Watts of power.

$$1000000000 / 86400 = 11000 \quad \text{(joules / seconds = watts)}$$

Your total energy use = Heating you + Moving you +
Feeding you + Housing you + Your stuff + Servicing you

KNOWN SOURCES OF ENERGY

by Dr. Saul Griffith

Scientists have been able to do a pretty good job of estimating where all the energy sources available to humans are and how much of each of them there are. Some of those resources are called fossil fuels: coal, oil, natural gas, and more recently we've added things like shale oil to that list. Fossil fuels are not infinite, and they are getting more expensive and harder to find and recover. It's time to look at the options. There is of course nuclear. Nuclear is considered 'non-renewable,' meaning we've got what we've got right now on Earth, and we ain't getting no more (unless we bring them in from asteroids or outer-space!). The other sources are called 'renewables,' which means we are always getting more of that energy coming into the Earth (from the sun and moon).

It is useful to step back and think about the energy sources that we've identified that we can use, and how they are made available on the Earth.

There are four kinds:

1. SOLAR ENERGY (renewable) which comes from nuclear fusion on the sun and manifests itself as light coming into Earth's atmosphere.

2. GRAVITATIONAL ENERGY (renewable) which comes from the gravitational pull of the moon on the Earth, and manifests itself as the energy in the ocean's tides as the water moves up and down.

3. HEAT ENERGY (Partly renewable, partly not) which is the heat energy stored in the Earth, remnant heat from the formation of the Earth billions of years ago as well as a little bit of heat from nuclear reactions in the Earth and (if you can imagine this) the heat created by the gravity of the moon squishing the Earth a little.

4. NUCLEAR (OR ATOMIC) **ENERGY** (not-renewable) which is the potential energy in the nuclear materials in the Earth's crust and core.

The sun itself will not 'burn' forever, so it's not exactly renewable, but as we are pretty confident it will burn for around five billion more years, it's not like we need to worry any time soon. Gravitational energy is renewable, probably forever, but quite honestly it is the least well understood and humans have only learned to harness the most trivial aspects of it (like apples falling from trees). Some of the heat energy is renewable (the gravity bit) but it's mostly going to cool down, albeit very very slowly — again, something we do not need to worry about for billions of years. The nuclear energy is most certainly not renewable; what we have on Earth now in the form of the various fissionable and fusion-able materials is all that we are going to get.

On Earth we can see where all of our energy comes from and relate it to these four sources.

We collect solar energy principally in the photons (sun rays) that make it all the way through the atmosphere and clouds, and are collected on photovoltaic panels, or in heating up water. There is more of this kind of energy than any other.

Solar energy also converts itself into wind energy by heating the atmosphere.

Solar energy is also converted into biomass, or plant matter, by photosynthesis and other biologic processes. Fossil fuels are in fact very very old solar energy that got converted into biomass, then converted into fossil fuels as it was buried and heated and pressurized for many millions of years.

Hydroelectricity is also solar energy, it turns out. Solar energy evaporates water that collects in clouds, that rains on mountains, that finds its way into dams, that can then be utilized.

Even the energy in the waves of the ocean is actually solar energy that becomes wind energy, that becomes wave energy as the wind blows over the surface of the water.

There's also a ton of heat in the world's oceans that can be harnessed that is solar energy that warmed up the top layer of the ocean.

Geothermal energy is how we can tap the heat energy stored in the Earth.

Nuclear energy comes in two types, fission (which is splitting large atoms into smaller ones) and fusion (which is making bigger atoms from smaller ones). Ultimately solar energy is fusion energy (so, in fact, the world is nuclear powered). Humans have figured out crude ways to harness the energy in fissionable materials, but we are still some way from elegantly being able to do what the sun does — fusion.

Tidal energy is pretty fascinating, and we know how to harness it, but sadly there just isn't that much. It's cool to imagine that the moon is producing this energy source here on Earth just by orbiting around the Earth!

Let's embark on a new path for our energy future.
- Dr. Saul Griffith

Measured in watts. Humans consume energy at the rate of 16 TW. By 2050 it is estimated to be 30 TW. We need more energy, these are our options.

FOUR KNOWN SOURCES OF ENERGY:

SOLAR

162,000 Terawatts [TW] RENEWABLE: INFINITE SOURCE

1 TW : 1000 Gigawatts [GW] *1 GW = 1 NUCLEAR REACTOR*
2 GW = 1 HOOVER DAM

1 TW : 1,000,000 Megawatts [MW] *1 MW = 1 WIND TURBINE*

1 TW : 1,000,000,000 Kilowatts [KW] *1 KW = 1 HORSEPOWER*

1 TW : 1,000,000,000,000 Watts [W] *100 W = 1 HUMAN*
1 W = 1 MOUSE

GRAVITY

FROM THE EARTH'S MOON: 3.7 TW

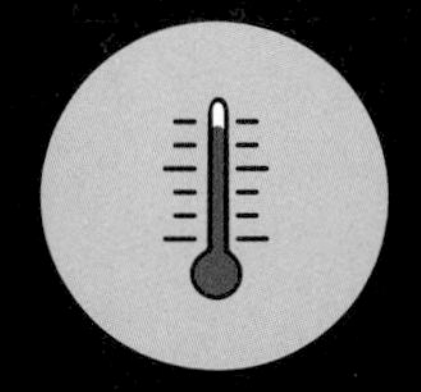

HEAT

FROM THE EARTH'S CORE: 32 TW

NUCLEAR

FROM THE EARTH'S CRUST: 1^{10} ZJ

NON-RENEWABLE: WILL RUN OUT!

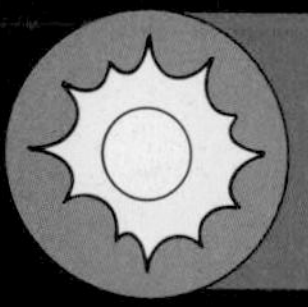

160,000 TW SOLAR ENERGY

SOLAR

31,000 TW ATMOSPHERIC ABSORBTION

RADIANT ENERGY GETS ABSORBED FROM THE SUN AND IS RETAINED INTO THE ATMOSPHERE. ENERGY CAN BE HARNESSED FROM THE WIND, OCEAN SURFACE WAVES, AND COASTAL WAVES.

WIND *CREATED BY THE SUN, CREATES...*

OCEAN SURFACE WAVES *MOVED BY THE WIND, CREATES...*

COASTAL WAVES

EARTH'S ATMOSPHERE

41,000 TW EVAPORATION

RADIANT ENERGY GETS EVAPORATED INTO THE ATMOSPHERE. CLOUDS CREATE RAIN, WHICH CREATES RIVERS USING GRAVITATIONAL ENERGY IS CONVERTED INTO HYDRO-ELECTRICITY.

HYDRO CLOUDS

HYDRO LAND

HYDRO RIVERS
HOOVER DAM (2 GW)

FOSSIL FUELS
COAL, NATURAL GAS, OIL, ETC.

BIOFUELS
WHEAT, CORN, ETC.

38,000 TW LAND & WATER HEATING

RADIANT ENERGY IS ABSORBED IN LAND AND WATER. THE LAND IS GENERALLY DARKER AND LESS REFLECTIVE THAN THE OCEAN AND WILL ABSORB MORE SOLAR RADIANT ENERGY INTO THE LAND SURFACE. THE OCEAN, REFLECTS A GREATER PORTION AND WILL ABSORB LESS.

WATER

LAND

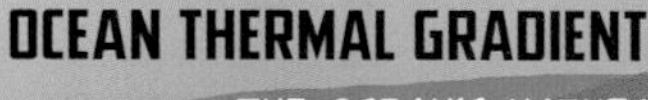

OCEAN THERMAL GRADIENT

THE OCEAN'S NATURAL THERMAL GRADIENT CAN GENERATE POWER WHEN THE WARMER SHALLOW SURFACE WATER MEETS WITH THE COOLER DEEPER WATER.

PHOTOSYNTHESIS

MUCH OF THE SUNLIGHT HITTING LAND IS ABSORBED BY PLANTS AND DRIVES PHOTOSYNTHESIS.

42,000 TW ATMOSPHERIC REFLECTION

SOLAR ENERGY REFLECTED FROM EARTH'S SURFACE, ATMOSPHERE, AND SCATTERING

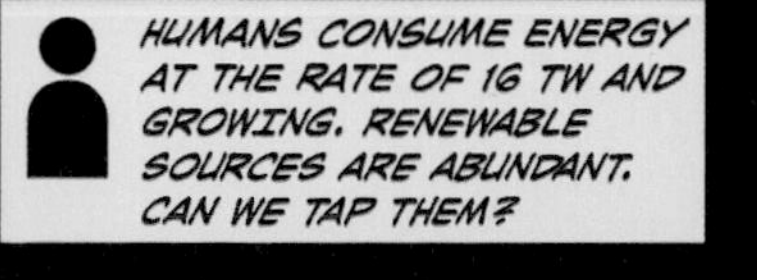

HUMANS CONSUME ENERGY AT THE RATE OF 16 TW AND GROWING. RENEWABLE SOURCES ARE ABUNDANT. CAN WE TAP THEM?

GRAVITY
3.7 TW MOON

ENERGY FROM THE GRAVITATIONAL PULL OF THE MOON IN THE FORM OF TIDAL.

NUCLEAR

1¹⁰ ZJ

A NON-RENEWABLE SOURCE FOUND IN THE EARTH'S CRUST. IT IS LEFTOVER MATERIALS FROM THE FORMATION OF THE UNIVERSE. INCLUDES PLUTONIUM, URANIUM, AND THORIUM.

CORE HAS ANCIENT HEAT FROM THE EARTH'S FORMING.

HEAT

32 TW

GEOTHERMAL: IS ENERGY STORED IN THE EARTH.

HISTORY OF ENERGY USE, PERSONAL AND GLOBAL. by Dr. Saul Griffith

Up until about 2000 years ago, humans really only knew how to tap three or four big energy sources: biofuels, solar energy, wind energy, and hydro power. We burned wood (biofuels) for heat, and captured solar energy in crops for food. Some people believe we were better at solar architecture 2000 years ago than we are today, and that many very, very old buildings had clever features for cooling and heating 'passively' with the sun and wind. The first uses of wind power were for sailing ships long distances (transportation) and for crushing grains. On a similar time frame, we learned to use hydro-power and built waterwheels that could also grind grains, operate saws and basic machinery, and do other useful work. The result was somewhat predictable; people didn't venture far from where they lived and they lived in small, efficient homes mostly heated by fireplaces. Proximity to flowing rivers, good sunlight, good soils and nearby forests were all good things to look for in a place to live. During this time, we invented things like the chimney and the root cellar. We didn't buy and own much stuff. Everything we ate was produced locally. Even so, in the early colonial days of the United States, we cut trees down at such a prolific rate that our energy use per person was comparable to today.

In the 19th century, we mastered making heat engines, and fossil fuels changed the world. People with names like Carnot and Watt figured out how to make steam engines that burned coal that powered the industrial revolution. Engines improved and Otto and Benz and other innovators made engines small enough and powerful enough to run cars, motorbikes, and then airplanes. This is when our energy consumption really took off. With cars we could travel much further, and we built highways and we built suburbs. By this time we had developed electricity networks that could feed power to those suburbs. Suburban houses grew larger and larger, and then we realized we could fill them with other amazing feats of energy engineering: the refrigerator, air-conditioning, all manner of cooking and entertainment devices. We learned to manufacture a great many things at an amazing global scale. Early in the 20th century we were harnessing all of the energy sources that we do today, and a bright guy called Einstein, ultimately much more famous for other things, did the initial work that led to atomic energy being viable, as well as the photovoltaic effect, now so critical in the modern solar industry. After World War II, we really ramped up production of all of this equipment including turbines, which were now the best way to power jet aircraft, as well as more efficient engines for stationary power plants. A dozen or so inventions had changed the entire world in a few hundred years. Some harnessed energy in new ways — photovoltaics, nuclear power plants, modern wind turbines — and many more used energy for new things — air conditioning, refrigeration, cars, airplanes. This is basically all of the stuff of modern life.

In Europe and America, all of these technologies took off quickly and successfully. In other parts of the world such as Asia, all of these benefits of high-energy living are just now being widely distributed. This is where the fastest-growing demand for energy is today. If everyone on the planet tried to live using the same amount of energy as an American or a European we would need to produce four to five times more energy than we do today. To say that would be hard is an understatement.

The big challenge is figuring out the right balance of all of the energy options. Any of the carbon fuels are pretty much a bad idea as they'll keep adding carbon to the atmosphere and raising the temperature of the planet. Wind is clean, but it's not very energy dense, meaning we need a lot of land with windmills on it to capture a little power. Hydro-electric is similar, and we are running out of good locations for it. Biofuels as they stand need huge amounts of land area. Solar is everywhere and comparatively energy dense compared to wind, but even so we need huge areas to be covered with solar energy collectors to create enough energy for humanity. This is why we still need to consider nuclear energy carefully as well as look to new options and research. Efficiency, or using energy wisely, is definitely very important, but it's not hugely popular as it often sounds like we need to do without — and who likes that? I think we should look at it differently and as an opportunity to more carefully choose the things that are important to us and to do them better.

Now is the moment in history to make all these decisions and embark on a new path for our energy future. Things have to change, and now is the moment to choose. Cheap prolific energy for the last few hundred years has shown us just how important energy is in terms of leading the lifestyles we wish to live. Renewable energy sources can provide all of the energy humanity needs, but whether we wish to cover that much land and whether the places we put it will be close enough or convenient to where we all want to live and when we all want the energy is the question that keeps people arguing about just which sources will power us into the future and how clean they will be. We can choose a beautiful future with enough energy for everyone, but we need to be smart.

LET'S INVENT THE FUTURE.

by Dr. Saul Griffith

When writing non-fiction, the fashion of the day is to write optimistic prose for a children's audience. When writing fiction for the same audience, the fashion is to craft the most destructive of dystopian disaster fantasies. We are guilty here of both of these charges, though our 'happy' ending is really only happy by contrast to the warped world of Dino Energy. In the real world, where we leave Tucker and Celine at the end of this story is only just the beginning. They've learned they must rebuild the infrastructure of the world around them to be a sustainable one that enables them to thrive. They've learned that every activity uses energy of some kind, that it is easy to waste energy, that it takes effort to harness energy, and that different forms of energy are more or less convenient. Our avid adventurers also learned that solar energy and its related renewable sources like wind energy are enormous pools of energy that we can easily tap into, and that are large enough for a plentiful supply for all of humanity.

Much as in the early chapters on Dino Energy, in the real world we blame someone else, a 'them' for the climate challenge It's so big and difficult-feeling that it is comforting in a way to imagine that 'they' were the problem, and that 'they' will fix it if the right incentives are put in place. The shortfall of this narrative with the energy and climate problem is that 'they' are us. We create the current enormous demand for energy by living the lives that we live. We don't wish to pay more for energy and hence we use too much of the cheapest, dirtiest energy sources: coal and oil. Because of the demand we create, markets and companies no more and no less sinister than Dino Energy fulfill our needs and give us those products, at the expense of the environment we all live in together.

So where is the hope? The fact that we are as much to blame as they are a hint. It also means that "we are the solution" is the headline. I believe, like in our story, that the future is in our children, in all of the Tuckers and Celines, with all of their ideas, inventions, and, yes, their energy. We won't solve our energy and climate challenges with small iterative changes. We won't merely change our lightbulbs to succeed. We need a sweeping big vision of the future that is more exciting, happier, and more desirable than what we have now. We then need to invent the technologies, lifestyles, economic systems, and even politics that will get us there. It's going to be rough and a little bit wild in parts because we'll need to reject some very established ways of doing things. It's going to be the best opportunity in a millennium for young people to rebel against the old ways of doing things. It's a great time to be young, contrary to opinion and headline, because there is great adventure in great change.

The current vision for our climate solution is to live largely like we do now, but to just substitute a few new technologies for some old ones. That's neither exciting, nor ambitious enough to truly meet the challenge. In the future, maybe we'll catch roller coasters to school. Everyone commuting in privately owned electric cars won't be as energy efficient and certainly not as thrilling as some out-of-the-box solution like a zipline network or an interconnected set of electric roller coasters. Goodbye stinkin' diesel bus! Goodbye school drop-off traffic jams! In the future, we'll arrive in style on electric skateboards and ziplines. The streets will be safer; the streets will in fact be different. We can reclaim them for playing football and hopscotch.

In the future we'll bow-hunt organic bison from electric monster trucks on Thursdays. The sustainable future is often presented as hygienic, almost boring in its bland success. All problems are solved, no adrenaline is necessary, every surface clean, every person the same. We can be more imaginative than that. We can satisfy our desires for adventure, thrills, beauty, culture, art, and environment in new and unusual ways. Why not imagine that we make our occasional hamburger a celebration and an all-day adventure instead of just a meal? Why don't we grow the cow (bison) in a more ethical way, so that it's healthier (organic) and then make a celebratory cultural event (bow hunt, electric monster truck) of the whole affair? And we can make it sustainable by making it a special event (Thursdays) rather than a constant daily over-consumption. Think really big and weird, and the future could really be interesting.

In the future, we'll be far healthier because we'll remove the perversions of the industrial food system with its reliance on energy as an input to agriculture, and we'll produce more food locally, and efficiently. Imagine that we can all be less fat because it is pleasant to be outside using your body more. Pick apples from tree-lined streets on your way to a friend's house. Imagine that we'll have less heart disease because we'll eat better. Imagine that we'll have fewer respiratory diseases and allergies because we'll clean up the air that we breathe. Imagine these things, then invent for us the pathways that will get us there. Be bold young people. Reject received wisdom. That received wisdom makes the sea levels rise.

In the future, more places will be beautiful, gardened, and vibrant with nature. We live in a world right now where we drive and travel great distances from beautiful place to beautiful place and wall ourselves in from the boring or ugly places in between. All this means too much flying, driving, riding, traveling and energy use. Rather than solve this problem by only thinking about changing the vehicles, we could turn the problem on its head, and make all of the places in between just as beautiful and just as interesting; then there would be less need to travel. We can do this with gardens and communities and pride in local places. It is possible to live in a lovely place where one can walk to work and ride to school and have parks at the end of every street to play and to exercise in. In short, we can build our infrastructure such that we rarely need to commute great distances. Dare to imagine skipping down a tree-lined forest pathway with dappled sunlight as your new commute. Think about that next time you are stuck on an on-ramp.

Let's not confuse things: what is at stake here is the quality of life we have on the planet we live on. We are warming the climate. The way we produce and use energy is to blame. Everything we do — whether it be toothbrushing, playing soccer, or driving to a holiday destination — uses energy, and because of the prevalence of our carbon-producing infrastructure, also produces carbon.

As with our delightfully whacky, inventive, and creative duo Tucker and Celine, be bold and imaginative about the opportunity that our energy and climate problem have given us. We are allowed to imagine some really creative solutions and futures. We are encouraged to reject the status quo and received wisdom. Go quickly, go creatively, and let's invent the future together.

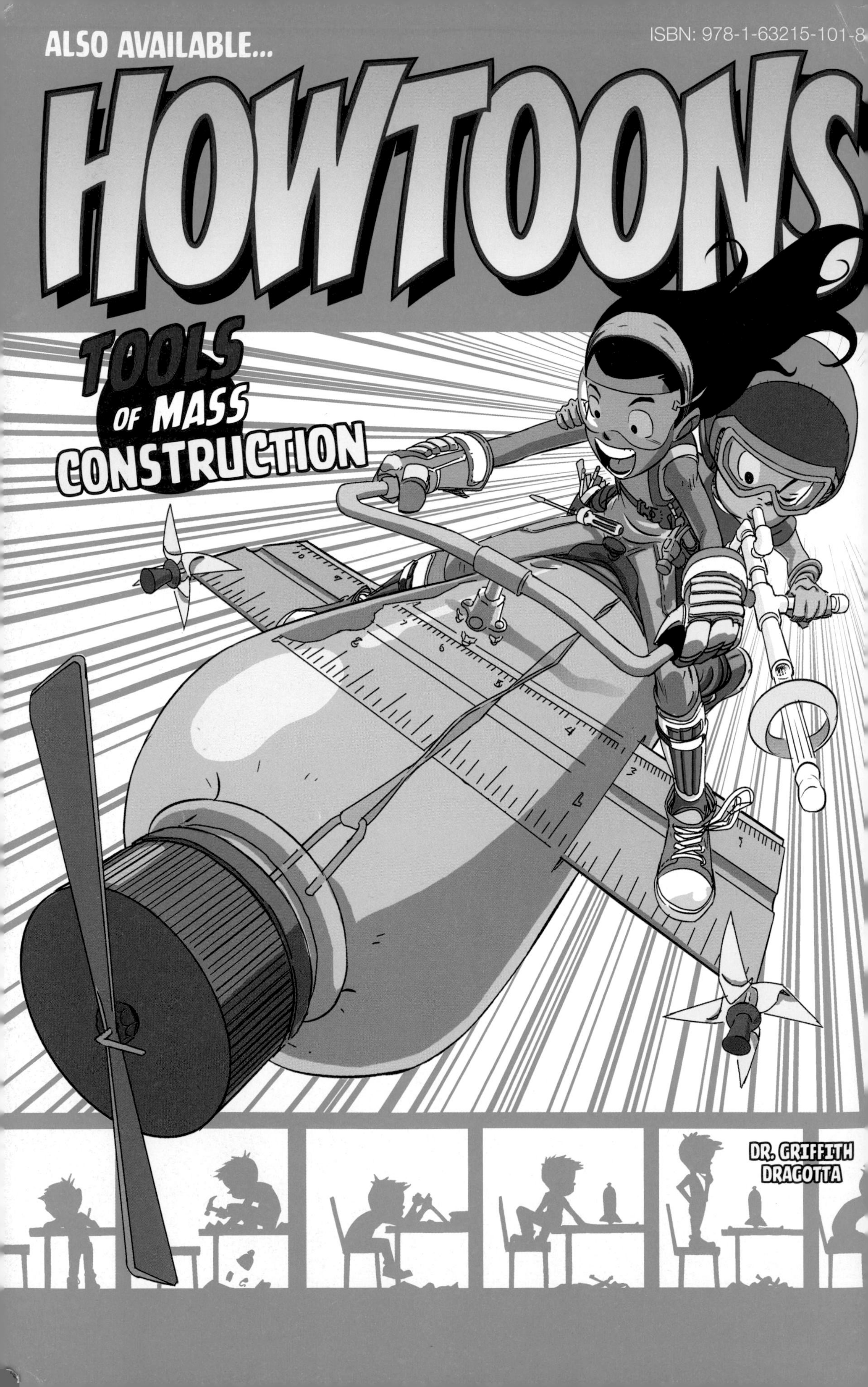
ALSO AVAILABLE...
ISBN: 978-1-63215-101-8
HOWTOONS
TOOLS OF MASS CONSTRUCTION
DR. GRIFFITH
DRAGOTTA

LURKING IN THE CORNERS OF YOUR GARAGE, THE DUSTY SHELVES OF HARDWARE STORES, AND YOUR OWN TRASH CAN ARE THE TOOLS AND INGREDIENTS FOR CREATING YOUR OWN ADVENTURES!
FOLLOW CELINE AND TUCKER AS THEY LEARN THE SECRETS OF MAKING THEIR OWN ENTERTAINMENT. CHALLENGED TO MAKE SOMETHING "OTHER THAN TROUBLE," THIS BROTHER AND SISTER PAIR USE EVERYDAY OBJECTS TO INVENT TOYS THAT YOU CAN BUILD.
SET UP A WORKSHOP. MAKE ICE CREAM WITHOUT A FREEZER. PLAY MUSIC WITH A TURKEY BASTER. LAUNCH ROCKETS AND MORE!
LEARN THROUGH PLAY!
OVER 360 PAGES CELEBRATING 10 YEARS OF HOWTOONS!

HOWTOONS
THE ENERGY OF THE WIND CAN RELEASE THE ROLLING POWER OF YOUR ... PAPER PLATE!
CAUTION
MAKING THIS SPEED DEMON CAN BE HAZARDOUS TO THE LAZY. ONCE IT'S RELEASED IN THE WIND, YOU'LL HAVE TO CHASE IT!

USE A PAPER PLATE TO CREATE.
CUT 8 SLICES IN THE INNER CIRCLE.
FOLD OUT EVERY OTHER SLICE.
LIKE SO.
PLACE THE PLATE ON THE GROUND AND WAIT FOR THE WIND TO PICK UP.
THE FOLD-OUT WINGS PROVIDE THE SURFACE FOR THE WIND TO PROPEL THE PLATE. THE GYROSCOPIC EFFECT OF ROTATION KEEPS IT BALANCED. THIS IS A SELF-BALANCING PAPER PLATE!
TRY DIFFERENT SIZES. SWAP OUT THE PAPER PLATE FOR A PIECE OF CARDBOARD. HOW BIG CAN YOU GO?!
ROLL ON!
DRAGOTTA '08

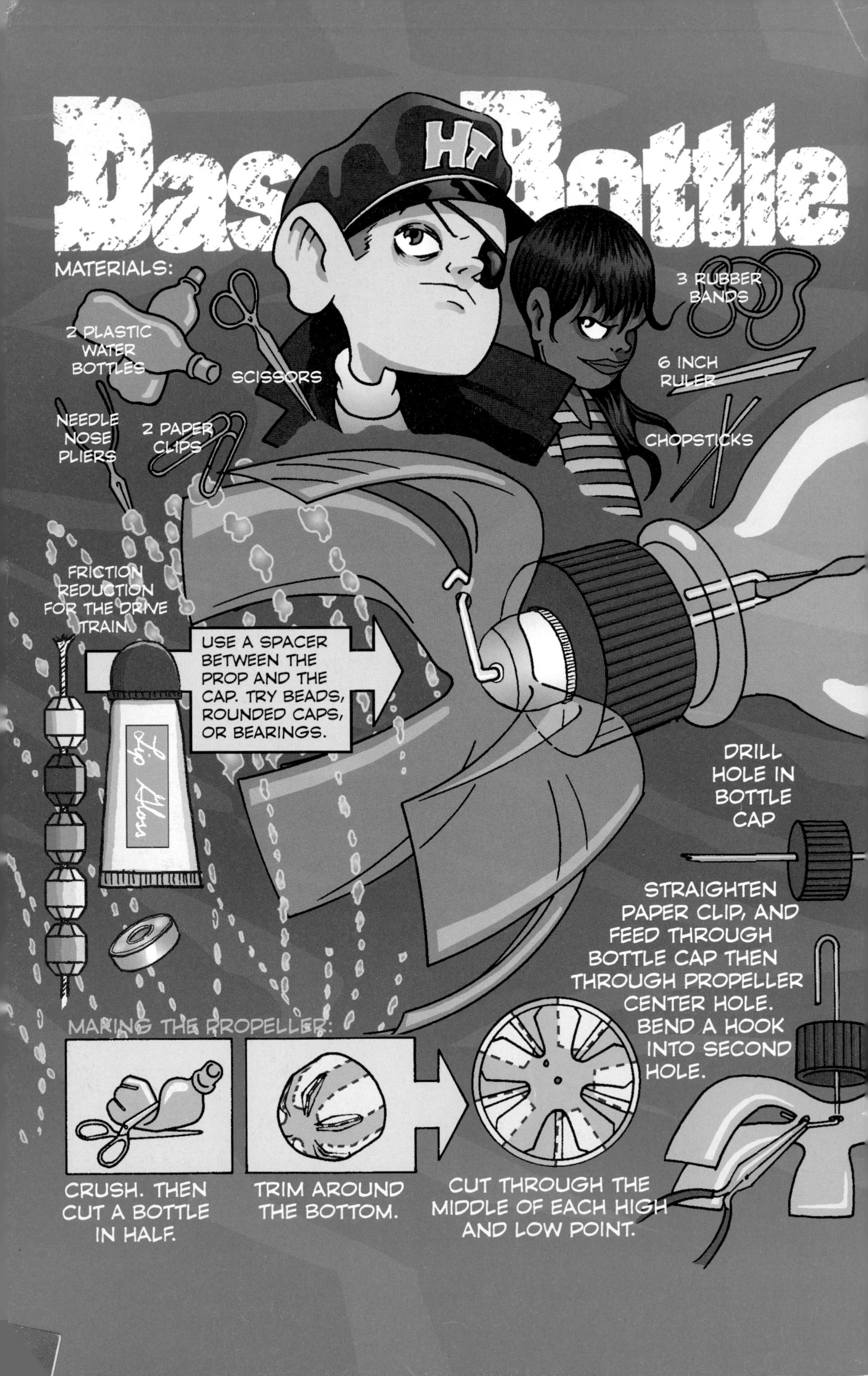
Das
Bottle
MATERIALS:
2 PLASTIC WATER BOTTLES
SCISSORS
3 RUBBER BANDS
6 INCH RULER
NEEDLE NOSE PLIERS
2 PAPER CLIPS
CHOPSTICKS
FRICTION REDUCTION FOR THE DRIVE TRAIN.
USE A SPACER BETWEEN THE PROP AND THE CAP. TRY BEADS, ROUNDED CAPS, OR BEARINGS.
DRILL HOLE IN BOTTLE CAP
STRAIGHTEN PAPER CLIP, AND FEED THROUGH BOTTLE CAP THEN THROUGH PROPELLER CENTER HOLE. BEND A HOOK INTO SECOND HOLE.
MAKING THE PROPELLER:
CRUSH. THEN CUT A BOTTLE IN HALF.
TRIM AROUND THE BOTTOM.
CUT THROUGH THE MIDDLE OF EACH HIGH AND LOW POINT.

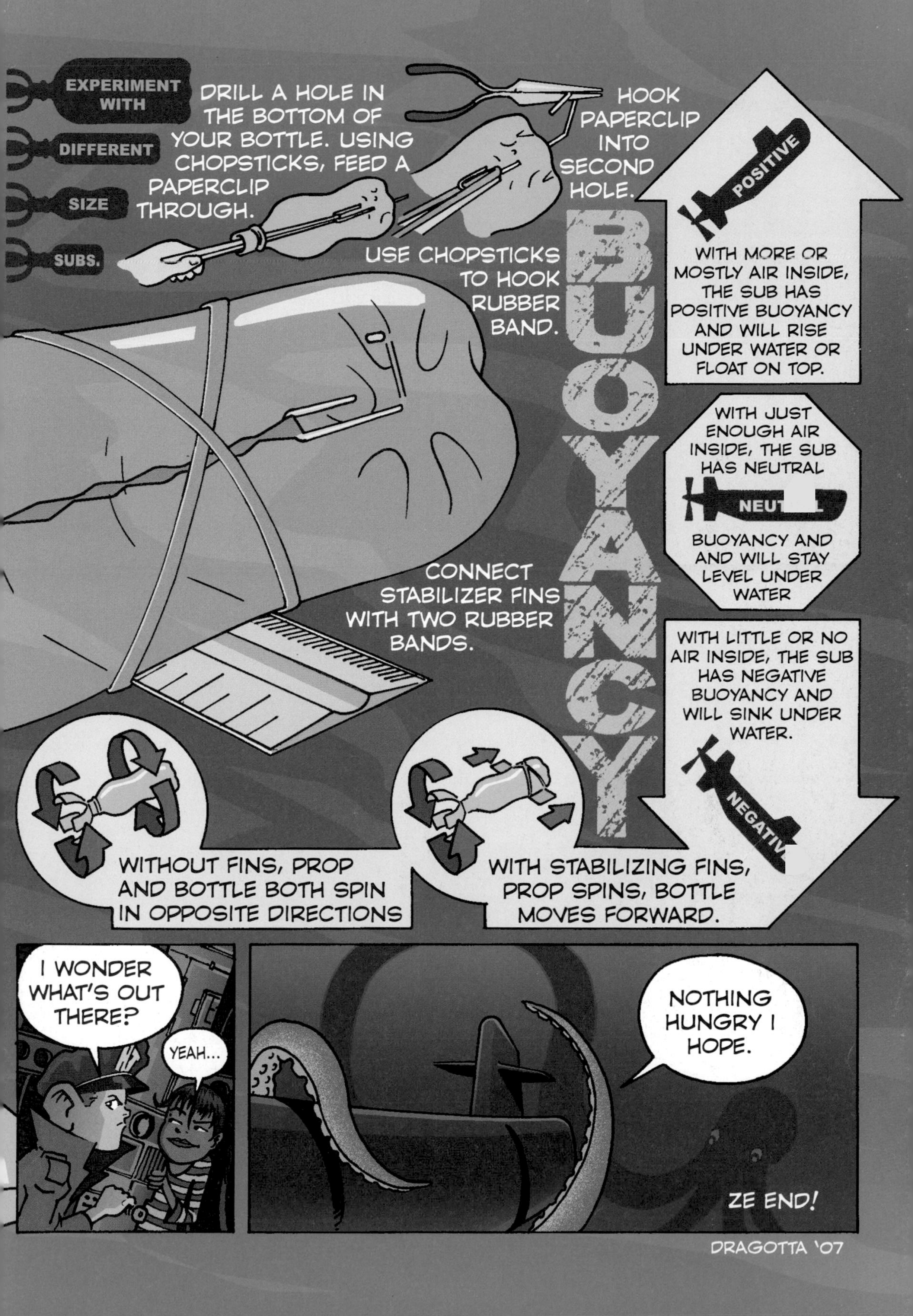

EXPERIMENT WITH
DIFFERENT
SIZE
SUBS.
DRILL A HOLE IN THE BOTTOM OF YOUR BOTTLE. USING CHOPSTICKS, FEED A PAPERCLIP THROUGH.
HOOK PAPERCLIP INTO SECOND HOLE.
USE CHOPSTICKS TO HOOK RUBBER BAND.
CONNECT STABILIZER FINS WITH TWO RUBBER BANDS.
BUOYANCY
POSITIVE
WITH MORE OR MOSTLY AIR INSIDE, THE SUB HAS POSITIVE BUOYANCY AND WILL RISE UNDER WATER OR FLOAT ON TOP.
WITH JUST ENOUGH AIR INSIDE, THE SUB HAS NEUTRAL
BUOYANCY AND AND WILL STAY LEVEL UNDER WATER
WITH LITTLE OR NO AIR INSIDE, THE SUB HAS NEGATIVE BUOYANCY AND WILL SINK UNDER WATER.
WITHOUT FINS, PROP AND BOTTLE BOTH SPIN IN OPPOSITE DIRECTIONS
WITH STABILIZING FINS, PROP SPINS, BOTTLE MOVES FORWARD.
I WONDER WHAT'S OUT THERE?
YEAH...
NOTHING HUNGRY I HOPE.
ZE END!
DRAGOTTA '07

HOWTOONS.COM

SMALL STEP FOR MAN

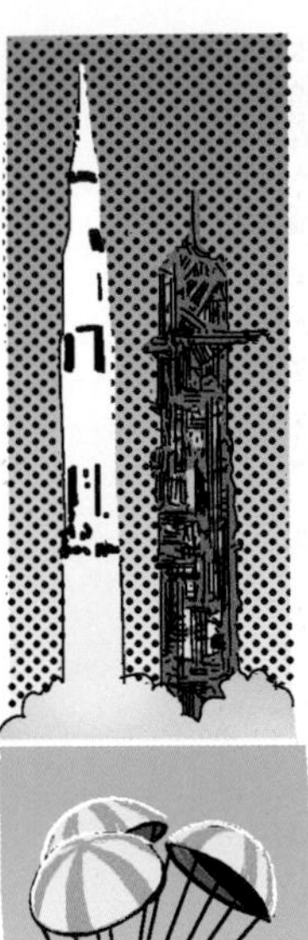

Toilet Paper

Alka-Seltzer

Cap

Pick up film canister at any local photo service center.

Film Canister
fill 1/4 with water

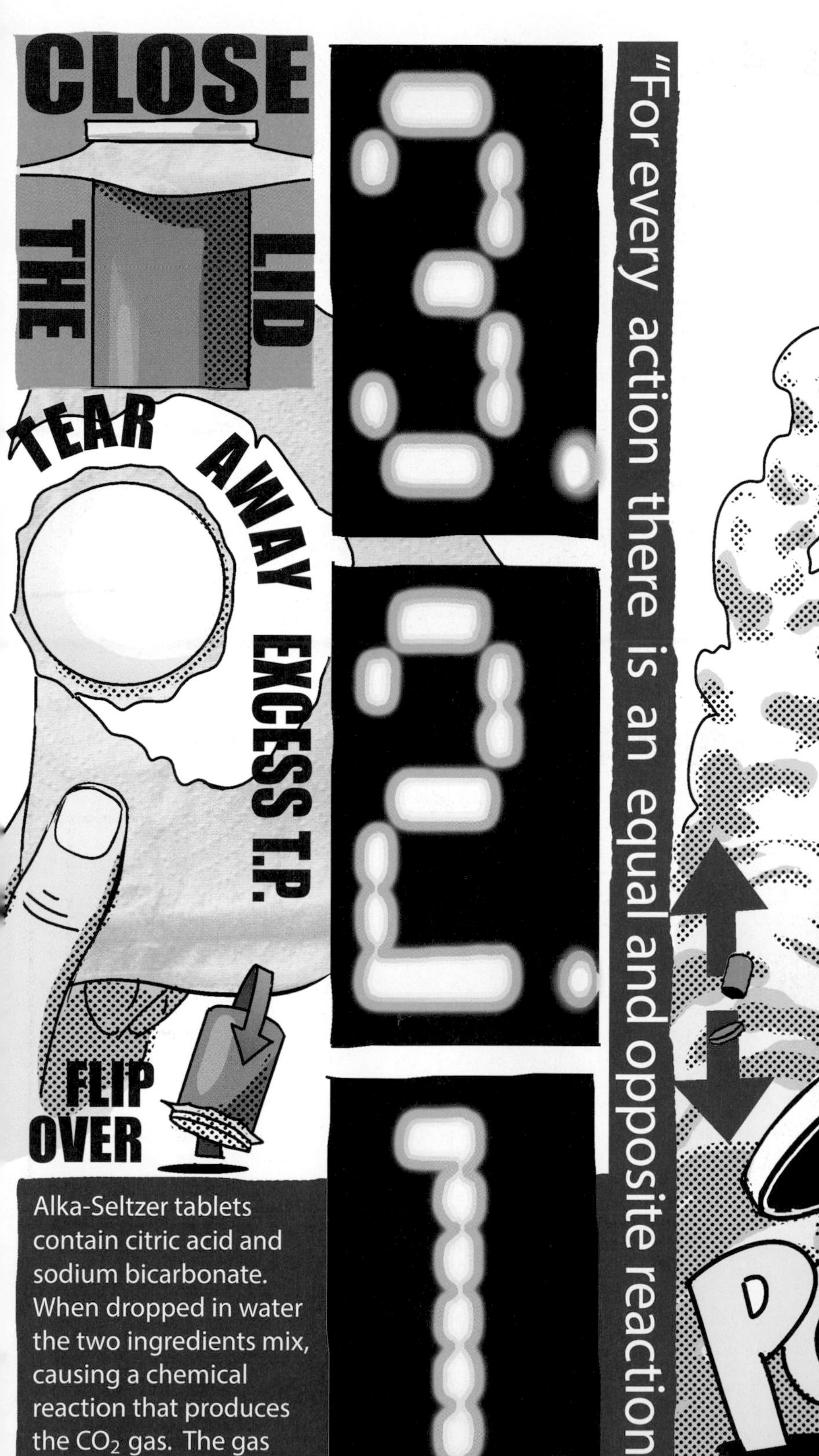
CLOSE THE LID
TEAR AWAY EXCESS T.P.
FLIP OVER
POP

Alka-Seltzer tablets contain citric acid and sodium bicarbonate. When dropped in water the two ingredients mix, causing a chemical reaction that produces the CO_2 gas. The gas builds until the bottle can't contain it anymore, thus Newton's 3rd law.

"For every action there is an equal and opposite reaction."

Sir Isaac Newton

HOWTOONS CREATOR BIOS

FRED VAN LENTE is the #1 NEW YORK TIMES-bestselling, award-winning writer of such non-fiction comics such as ACTION PHILOSOPHERS (an American Library Association Best Graphic Novel for Teens), THE COMIC BOOK HISTORY OF COMICS, and the upcoming ACTION PRESIDENTS. He also likes to make stuff up, as evidenced by ARCHER & ARMSTRONG (2014 Harvey Award nominee, Best Continuing Series), RESURRECTIONISTS, BRAIN BOY, AMAZING SPIDER-MAN, GI JOE, and COWBOYS & ALIENS, the basis for the feature film. He lives in Brooklyn with his wife, the playwright Crystal Skillman, and some mostly ungrateful cats.

As a cartoonist and illustrator **TOM FOWLER** has worked in comics, advertising, and film and game design. He has worked for Disney, Simon & Schuster, Wizards of the Coast, Hasbro, MAD, Valiant, Marvel, and DC Comics. His best known comics include the MAD MAGAZINE feature "MONROE", VENOM, HULK SEASON ONE, and the critically acclaimed MYSTERIUS THE UNFATHOMABLE. Tom lives and works in Ottawa with his wife Monique, and this book's core demographic Graham, who also fights robot dinosaurs on a fairly regular basis.

JORDIE BELLAIRE is an Eisner Award-winning Colorist best known for her Image projects, MANHATTAN PROJECTS, NOWHERE MEN, PRETTY DEADLY, AUTUMNLANDS: TOOTH & CLAW, and ZERO. She lives in Ireland with her bossy cat, Buffy and drinks lots of coffee.

A comic letterer since 2003, **RUS WOOTON** is best known for his work on books such as THE WALKING DEAD, INVINCIBLE, THE BOUNCE, EAST OF WEST, MANHATTAN PROJECTS, BLACK SCIENCE, DEADLY CLASS, and many others. He currently resides in Denver, Colorado and subsists on coffee, spicy Korean noodles, and the occasional Dr Pepper.

HOWTOONS was originally created by scientists **SAUL GRIFFITH**, **JOOST BONSEN**, and artist **NICK DRAGOTTA** out of MIT. The team was later joined by toy designer **INGRID DRAGOTTA**. The Howtoons goal is to engage kids with science, art, engineering, and all the related disciplines through the language of comics, inspiring hands-on play and learning.